Liberty schools

A Parent's Voucher Plan
A NEW WAY TO HANDLE SCHOOL MONEY

by R. J. Lytle

STRUCTURES PUBLISHING COMPANY
FARMINGTON, MICHIGAN   1975

Manufactured in the United States of America.

Book designed by Richard Kinney.

Current Printing (last digit)
10 9 8 7 6 5 4 3 2 1
International Standard Book Number: 0-912336-15-3
Library of Congress Catalog Card Number: 75-17039

Structures Publishing Company
Box 423, Farmington, Michigan 48024

liberty schools

To: Marilyn, Bob Jr., Anne, Peter, Jeanne, Andy, Katie, Mark, Jenny and Margaret—that schools may improve for them and for their children.

"Perhaps the sentiments contained in the following pages are not *yet* sufficiently fashionable to procure them general favor; a long habit of not thinking a thing *wrong* gives it a superficial appearance of being *right,* and raises at first a formidable outcry in defense of custom. But the tumult soon subsides. Time makes more converts than reason."

Thomas Paine, "Common Sense", 1776

CONTENTS

Preface

PERSONS WHO HAVE benefited financially from our democratic freedoms, as have professional people, doctors, lawyers, corporate executives and businessmen, have a moral obligation to participate in civic affairs, preserving and extending those freedoms. Failure to do so would abdicate the responsibility of government to professional politicians whose motives and objectives frequently differ from those of the public as a whole.

What better civic activity for a man with ten children, than schools?

This decision being made, there followed many years of involvement in school affairs, PTA, Study Committees, and Millage Committees, and a candidacy for the school board. Meanwhile, I read extensively on the subject of schools and education.

I watched as school boards agonized over the most minute decisions; decisions that should be in the province of a minor official. I was startled to find that some of the most serious problems were resolved not on the basis of facts, and benefits to children, but on fear of criticism.

Although I found that I could accomplish some improvement (and I have) by working within the system, writing letters to the editor, etc., change was slow, small and sometimes overwhelmed by bureaucratic inertia. At the same time, I became convinced that educators knew more about the technical side of their profession than any parent had time to learn. However, the organization of schools for the job they were supposed to accomplish was the cause of much inefficiency and was inherited from a time when schools were primarily rural. It was here that I thought I could make a contribution.

When I first began writing about these ideas, I arranged a meeting with the business agent of the local teachers' union. His first comment was: "Bob, what background do you have that qualifies you to write about schools?" Now that's a good question. First and perhaps foremost, I am a customer of schools, and a very sizable one at that! I do not have enough years left to learn what I should know in order to write about education with the insight of George Dennison, Mario Fantini, Paul Goodman, Colin Greer, John Holt, Christopher Jencks, Jonathan Kozol, Charles Silberman and others.

But as a consumer of education services, I do have the right to speak my mind, and it is from this perspective that I write. For example, builders like myself have long been subject to constraints imposed by nonbuilders (including educators). The nonbuilders do not attempt to tell us how we should construct the house but we are subject to building codes, zoning laws, safety regulations, etc., all imposed by nonbuilders. So as a noneducator, I will make no attempt to tell educators about cognitive and affective domain; about team-teaching vs. the open classroom, etc., but I do insist on my say regarding organization and financing and my right to choose among available schools.

I became convinced that the primary needs of schools were more freedom and diversity even before reading about the voucher system of education. If we could give each principal some autonomy, I thought, then those principals offering the best and most effective program would attract more pupils and the school-closing dilemma,* which was

---

*Enrollment had drastically declined from a 1967 peak. One school had been closed, accompanied by much discord, and three more were planned to be closed.

the central problem in our district, would solve itself.

To this end, I wrote a series of articles for our suburban newspaper. The thrust of these articles was not a full voucher system, but a limited plan which would permit parents to choose any school in two adjoining districts, Birmingham and Bloomfield Hills. I felt that it might be possible to have some of the benefits of free choice without waiting for public interest to be aroused and legislative action. Some of the material in this book is an outgrowth of that series of articles, and is included here with the permission of the Observer-Eccentric Newspapers.

I began to realize that the Liberty School** idea, if it were ever to become a reality, must have more going for it than diversity and competition. So my intent is to show that Liberty Schools will provide answers for groups with such diverse aims as integrated schools, religious schools, private schools, neighborhood schools, individual teacher freedom, the revitalization of higher education, preparation for future changes in schools, and last but not least, the increase of personal freedoms.

Some of the ideas proposed are new and most are controversial. At the expected expense of being accused of being simplistic, I have tried to keep the book simple, avoiding educational jargon. Simple, but not simplistic, which means ignoring of the complexities of a problem. The following proposal will counter most educators' charges of being "simplistic" by presenting in great detail a plan that recognizes its evolutionary nature, and offers both gradual and complete solutions to many of our current education problems.

** A practical realization of the voucher theory, recognizing the many problems facing schools.

1. Introduction

THE LIBERTY PLAN is designed to improve schools by a practical realization of the voucher theory of free choice in education. The theory gives the tax money used for education to parents, and allows them a choice of schools. The Liberty plan may enable us to turn the multitude of serious problems facing schools today into opportunities for constructive change.

These problems range from integration to enrollment decline, teacher militancy, lack of funds, and inefficiency, and can cause ruinous developments. But we can harness these forces for change to create basic, constructive alterations in the operation of schools from kindergarten to graduate school. While responding to the problems, we can implement long-needed improvements in schools. At the same time, we can structure schools to facilitate changes for the future. Central to this idea is the provision of diverse schools, responsive to individual learning needs.

Students, like adults, vary in their emotional makeup, intelligence, aptitudes and family background. These characteristics determine whether the student will learn best in a structured, teacher-directed classroom; in an open, self-directed environment, or somewhere in between. We can call this "learning style." Each student's learning style and educational needs are different. Parents need schools that are compatible with the learning styles of their families. Even within a family, the need for a different school for each child may become evident.

Each individual has a different concept of both the purpose of schools and the methods they should employ.

The strife and dissension presently surrounding schools are the result of limited choice on the part of parents, teachers and students. Education will improve and much of this antagonism and conflict avoided, if we agree to permit a free choice of schools within our educational system. If the taxpayers' money, now given to school boards, is given directly to parents to be spent on schools, free choice can be realized. We call this system "Liberty Schools."

Two of the most abrasive school conflicts stem from forced busing to achieve racial integration, and rejection by religious groups of certain books or theories which seem to them contrary to their religious beliefs. But if each of us is willing to recognize the rights of others to a choice of school programs, then even such major disputes can be resolved.

Among the schools available in many cities are traditional, progressive or open schools. Good conduct may mean obedience in the first, cooperation in the second, and uninhibited self-expression in the last. Mini schools, or school within a school, can offer variety within the same building. Year-round, religious, and neighborhood schools can be offered in response to parental demand. Parents are competent to choose, and to make the decision effective a transportation plan, minimizing the use of scarce fuel, can be developed using existing urban transportation and shuttle buses. The purpose of the transportation would not be to force integration, although this would occur and be a desirable by-product, but to improve opportunities for those seeking a better education.

Education research, notably by Christopher Jencks, et al, in *Inequality*,[1] indicates that the public and children are ill served by homogenized schools. Since it is not known what effect the character of a school has on the child's eventual achievement or outlook, our society cannot impose uniformity on schools on socially moral grounds. Nor should educators have the authority to rule out schools which appeal to parents even though they do not meet the "standards" of the profession.

Funds supplied by taxes would be redistributed to the parents in the form of a voucher restricted to use in schools meeting certain minimal state instruction standards. This system would add some elements of free market competition, with the result that schools would become more responsive to the needs of students, thus becoming more efficient and effective.

The declining birth rates that have prevailed for some years have made school vacancies the rule rather than overcrowding. These lower enrollments improve our opportunity to provide an effective choice of schools. With the geographic density of schools in metropolitan areas and the availability of transportation, there is little real reason why all students, but particularly the poor and racial minorities, cannot be given a wide choice of schools without force once the restrictions of artificially created school-attendance boundaries have been eliminated. At the same time, schools responsive to a wide range of religious beliefs can come into being and can be attended with less difficulty.

The first mention of education vouchers came from Adam Smith, the economist, about the time of the American Revolution. Parents were to be given money to pay a schoolmaster, once they were satisfied with his work.

John Stuart Mill in his classic *On Liberty* (1859) was concerned about keeping government out of education. This led him to suggest a voucher system for education, to help poor families while preventing state control of the curriculum.

Probably the man most responsible for the current interest in education vouchers is Milton Friedman, the

University of Chicago economist. A chapter in his book, *Capitalism and Freedom*,[2] published in 1962, criticizes the government's role in providing education services:

> But let a poor family in a slum have a gifted child and let it set such high value on his or her schooling that it is willing to scrimp and save for the purpose. Unless it can get special treatment, or scholarship assistance, at one of the very few private schools, the family is in a very difficult position. The 'good' public schools are in the high income neighborhoods. The family might be willing to spend something in addition to what it pays in taxes to get better schooling for its child. But it can hardly afford simultaneously to move to the expensive neighborhood.

The GI bill, which gives veterans an education entitlement, is a highly successful voucher example. Funds may be spent at a wide variety of institutions, public, private or religious colleges, vocational schools, etc.

Liberty Schools would provide parents with a voucher with which they could pay for a year's schooling at any school in the state. The system would be a state responsibility. Federal funds could be channeled to the schools but only through the state's voucher machinery.

The dollar value of the Liberty School voucher would be the same throughout the state but with different values for the various grade levels: kindergarten, elementary, junior high, high school and college or higher education. Additional vouchers would be issued for the retarded, children with learning disabilities, and others with recognized needs.

Vouchers, until used, would retain their value throughout the lifetime of the student. This would permit the student to return to school at any time to complete programs or take additional courses. Vouchers could increase in value over the years, with the cost of living, or changes in public policy. For example, if the student drops out at the end of the eleventh grade, his twelfth grade voucher can be used any time during his lifetime, for any education purpose, at the value in effect at the time of use.

The total value of all vouchers in the state would not exceed the present total expenditures for education. Tax sources could be the same as at present, Federal, state and local, or different sources of revenue could be used. Schools would be the present public school system and, under some circumstances, private or religious schools.

A limited experiment with vouchers started in 1972 in the poor and largely Spanish-American school district of Alum Rock at San Jose, California. The experiment includes only public schools with additional funding from a federal grant of $1,586,000.00. Only six of the district's 24 schools voluntarily participated in 1972 to 1973, but seven more joined the program in the 1973 to 1974 school year for an enrollment of 9000. Despite the limited and regulated nature of the demonstration, 84% of participating teachers and 80% of the parents were pleased with the program at the end of the first year.

California is not the only state to experiment with voucher schools. New Hampshire plans a more effective experiment when a federal grant can be obtained. Unlike Alum Rock, the New Hampshire program will include private nonsectarian schools. Parents will be allowed to provide additional tuition, should they wish to send their children to a school charging more than the publicly provided voucher. As in Alum Rock, federal funds will be used as incentive grants. William P. Bittenbender, Chairman of the New Hampshire Board of Education, speaks of the program:

In the process, hopefully, a great deal of the political heat generated at the local school district level will have been dissipated. This can be achieved by offering those citizens previously discontented with the boards' and administrators' rules as directors of the specific educational form a freer education choice in a more competitive market of public and private school suppliers of education. . . . Unanimity is hard to achieve among free men whose choice is limited. But when agreement can be obtained to allow and provide for diversity; to minister to as many specific value systems and goals as is financially feasible; unanimity of resolve may not be far behind.

Spending money in addition to that which is already provided for schools is not necessary and may, in fact, impede the changes in schools recommended here. *The Greening of the High School,*[3] a report by the Educational Facilities Laboratory, makes this point:

> Money, it was felt, is overrated as an instrument of change. It doesn't require federal funding to initiate a program in ecology or consumer education, to offer relevant curriculum, or out of school programs. What it takes is getting people to stop what they do habitually, and do something else. This doesn't mean that change is always possible without money, but the prevailing attitude which says, 'money first and then we'll produce change' is diversionary. There is no record to support the view that dollars, whether they come from the government or private philanthropy, provide an effective way to approach reform in the United States.
>
> Moreover, there is an illusion about *how much* money it costs for new approaches. Evidence indicates that if people care about what they're doing, they will devote endless hours and make sacrifices—a factor that breeds the respect not only of the students, but of the community as well.

We now have public, private and church-related schools. What types of elementary and secondary schools would be available when the Liberty plan is in effect? The formerly public schools would be called *independent.* These schools, in general, would continue to operate as they do now. However, they would have no geographical limitations or boundaries. As independent schools, they would have no prohibition against religious instruction and may, if their patrons wish, offer optional religious courses.

Present church-related schools would be much as they are now except that they would be able to cash vouchers. A religion-oriented curriculum would be the main difference from the independent schools.

The present private schools, should they elect to joint the Liberty system, would not differ basically from the independent schools. They would have the same governance, traditions they now have, and would be oriented toward the same type of student now enrolled.

All schools would be subject to the same minimum state standards for safety and instruction. Discrimination would be prohibited. The school may charge more than the voucher, if they wish, but would then be required to provide scholarships to the poor as described in Chapter 3.

In higher education, the Liberty plan would increase the equity of our funding distribution; increase the cost-effectiveness of these institutions, public and private; put an end to the serious discrimination we practice by requiring diplomas and degrees as credentials for employment and promotion; and, by freeing these schools from reliance on an artificial market, enable schools to respond to the unmet knowledge needs of young and old without regard to artificial, credential considerations.

So far we have presented the Liberty School theory in broad terms. Its advantages to the student are many:

the creation of diverse schools to match the child; the furthering of racial integration by providing access to better schools for any child, regardless of color or economic class; the enabling of optional moral or religious training in the now-public schools; and the provision of financial support for church-related education, without an increase in taxes.

For teachers, Liberty Schools will provide the freedom to choose a school having a teaching philosophy compatible with their own; superior teachers can be paid more for outstanding work; thousands of teachers can be provided employment through an add-on tuition feature; and teacher militancy can be redirected to cooperation with school managers who have the authority to satisfy parent customers.

Further, the Liberty School can, by providing a competitive climate, improve the effectiveness and consumer responsiveness of schools; permit neighborhood schools becoming surplus by virtue of declining enrollment to be closed by parental choice, not administrative edict; and open the door to new potentials in the future of education.

Finally, Liberty Schools will increase personal freedoms by moving an activity involving one third of the population and what is now one quarter of government spending, into private hands. The following chapters will deal with the details of how the plan can be made to work, and possible complications and objections which may arise and ways to overcome them.

2. Voucher Plans and Experiments

EDUCATION VOUCHERS ARE defined as a certificate representing a sum of money issued by a public agency to parents for the education of their children. In the first chapter we took a brief look at the history of the voucher idea. Now we must consider some of the details of various voucher proposals and how experimental plans have worked or are planned to work. We can then compare these proposals with the Liberty plan.

Voucher education is new and different in that the public money which now goes to schools directly would, if a voucher system were adopted, go to the parents and then to the school. This would allow parents to choose schools, and add some elements of free-market competition, resulting in schools that were more responsive to the needs of students, and more efficient and effective educational tools.

The way schools are presently organized, with standard, homogenized programs, the only way one group of parents can have their curriculum or schedule proposals adopted is at the expense and dissatisfaction of another group of parents. If the first group of parents has its way, the result is the imposition of its ideas on the second group. So the normal situation is a constant war between competing groups. A voucher plan would enable the parent groups to satisfy their differing requirements and thus provide a better, less hostile, learning environment.

If it were possible for parents to finance the cost of schools themselves, without help from the public purse, it would be most desirable. However, that is not the case. If parents were to pay for schools, schools used by poor families might be of poor quality or nonexistent. Furthermore, the public and the tax structure have grown accustomed to financing nearly all schools with tax money, and this is not likely to change.

Only the very rich now have a choice of schools. They can ignore the substantial school taxes they pay and send their children to private schools. Another way they exercise a choice of schools is by moving to a community with a reputation for excellence in schools. Thus, an executive for a major corporation being transferred to a post in a new city often decides the location of his home by the quality of the schools. Most of us, however, do not have this economic freedom of choice. We must take whatever the local school district has to offer, within a restricted enrollment area. This need not be.

Another advantage the voucher system has over other proposals to change schools is that it permits continual change as opposed to periodic upheavals. Thus, as we learn more about the art of education, improvements in techniques will come on-stream faster.

In the first chapter, we quoted Milton Friedman of the University of Chicago as one of the modern proponents of a voucher system of education. Here is a further quotation from his book, *Capitalism and Freedom:*[2]

> The parent who would prefer to see money used for better teachers and texts rather than coaches and corridors has no way of expressing this preference except by persuading a majority to change the mixture for all. This is a special case of the general principle that a market permits each to satisfy his own taste—effective proportional representation; whereas the political process imposes conformity. In addition, the parent who would like to spend some extra money on his child's education is greatly

limited. He cannot add something to the amount now being spent to school his child and transfer his child to a more costly school. If he does transfer his child, he must pay the whole cost and not simply the additional cost. He can only spend extra money easily on extra-curricular activities—dancing lessons, music lessons, etc. Since the private outlets for spending more money on schooling are so blocked, the pressure to spend more on the education of children manifests itself in ever higher public expenditures on items ever more tenuously related to the basic justification for governmental intervention into schooling.

Professor Friedman expanded further on his voucher ideas in a 1973 article in the New York Times Magazine. He compares the operation of schools and grocery stores:

A fable may dramatize the true source of the nation's present discontent with our public schools: Suppose that, 50 or 75 years ago, the U.S. had adopted the same institutional arrangements for the distribution of food as it did adopt for elementary and secondary schools. Suppose, that is, that the retail provision of groceries had been nationalized, that food was paid for by taxes and distributed by Government-run stores. Each family would be assigned to a store, as it is now assigned to a school, on the basis of its location. It would be entitled to receive, without direct payment, a collection of foods, as its children are entitled to receive a collection of classes. It would be able to choose among foods, as its children choose among subjects. Presumably this would be done by giving each family some number of ration points and assigning point prices to various foods. Private grocery stores would be permitted (just as private schools are), but persons shopping in them would be taxed for the support of the public stores just the same.

Can there by any doubt what retail food distribution would be like today if this system had been in effect? Would there be supermarkets and chain stores? Would the shelves be loaded with new and improved convenience products? Would stores be using every device of human ingenuity to attract and retain customers?

Suppose that under such a system you were unhappy with your local grocery. You could not simply go to a different store unless you were able and willing to pay twice for your groceries, once in taxes and again in cash. No, you would have to work through political channels to change the elected or appointed Grocery Board, or the Mayor, or the Governor, or the President. Obviously, this would be a cumbrous, inefficient process. And suppose you had different ideas from your neighbors about the kind of service you wanted? What then? You would have to find a neighborhood of like-minded people to which you could move.

Friedman goes on to describe a voucher plan similar to the Liberty plan, but lacking the 5% scholarship requirement, which is detailed in the following chapter. This would require those schools charging more than the public voucher to have 5% of enrollment in scholarships for the poor. This feature would overcome the objections of those concerned that the poor would suffer under a voucher plan.

Not surprisingly, a number of university professors were quick to take issue with Friedman on his School/Grocery example. They accused him of turning over schools to private enterprise. This, of course, is not what either of us propose. We simply want competition among the present and public schools. Another letter abhors the idea that parents could know what is educationally "best" for their children. The letter adds that "both professional analysis and collective social judgment" are required to determine what children should learn. To the last accusation, Friedman responds:

> The alleged incompetence of parents is an argument against the voucher plan only on the implicit assumption (a) that someone else is more competent and (b) should be given the right to decide, whether parents agree or not. Without assumption (b) there's nothing to prevent parents from seeking advice, as we all do in a wide range of fields. . . . Assumption (b) reflects an elitist anti democratic view which denigrates 'them' and says that 'we' should be put in charge. After all 'we' know better than 'they' what is good for 'them.' This is to promote aristocracy while preaching democracy.

We can add that subsequent education research, by Christopher Jencks and others, indicates that parents can and do make valid choices for their children. Jencks is one of the directors of the Center for the Study of Public Policy, in Cambridge, Massachusetts. The Center developed a "Regulated, Compensatory Voucher Plan" in 1969 under contract with the Office of Economic Opportunity. The plan was to be used for demonstrations of the feasibility of voucher programs in several communities.

Features of the regulated model include:

1. *Public voucher must be full payment for tuition.* This provision deprives parents of the opportunity to spend more on schools if they so desire. It would not contribute to increased teacher employment nor would it give the poor an opportunity to attend expensive schools through the Liberty 5% scholarship provision.

2. *The school must accept any applicant as long as it has vacant spaces.* This would deprive the school of the freedom to structure their program for students with a certain learning style, without discrimination as to race or affluence.

3. *If the school has more applicants than spaces, pick half of them by lot and the other half in a nondiscriminatory manner.* We can comment the same as on number 2, above. Also, the report published in 1970 still assumes that crowded schools are the norm rather than the present, declining enrollment, situation.

Once any group in our society has achieved such dominance over an activity as educators have over schools, it is difficult to sever the bonds. This is demonstrated in the case of this regulated voucher plan which professes to provide freedom but actually continues, even reinforces, bureaucratic control. While it attempts to improve opportunities for disadvantaged children, it does this with condescension. The report speaks of educational goals "which we think are important." The *we* in this case is not the poor, or the great mass of parents, but Professors of Education.

The Center has not been successful in persuading any community, except California's Alum Rock School District, to agree to demonstrate its "regulated" model. Even at Alum Rock, many modifications were made to suit local parents and staff.

At Alum Rock, only the data from the first year (72-73) of a five- to seven-year demonstration is now available. The Rand Corporation studied the Alum Rock schools and concludes, "This first year report must be taken for what it is—a description of a newborn educational program in its first year of life. The course of the program's development and the possibilities for healthy and independent growth are still uncertain."[14]

The diversity of the schools was largely the result of the creation of mini-schools, or schools within a school. There were 22 of these in the six schools of the first year, and 45 in the 13 schools in the second year. This is not to say that there were 45 different programs because many programs were similar from school to school. Most children attended the same school they did the year before, and there was no increase in segregation, as had been feared by some critics.

Of the 22 elementary mini-schools in the six first year voucher schools, 11 were classed as basic academic; two concentrated on reading; one on math; two emphasized fine arts; two learned about different cultures; and four taught basic academic skills through practical, everyday activities.

Teachers frowned on competition, however, and when one mini-school received some modest publicity in a local newspaper some teachers regarded it as unfair advertising. The Rand Report comments further:

> A public school system is unlikely to develop schools or mini-schools that are competitive and independent for at least the first few years of a voucher demonstration without strong outside pressures. Teachers and administrators are likely to succeed in preventing such competition, because
> - They regard competition as unethical and unprofessional.
> - They see it as a threat to job security, despite any new protective guarantees, because it establishes a potentially dangerous new precedent with unpredictable long-run consequences.

• The movement of students between schools or mini-schools makes it hard to plan, since educational planning as now practiced depends on predictable student enrollment and budgets.

On the other hand, strong outside pressures to expand competition in a public school system may well produce an organized reaction, encouraging demonstration participants to cooperate against those pressures, which would threaten the existing stability. In Alum Rock, the six voucher principals, rather than competing with one another for students, cooperated against the central voucher staff, which was trying to implement some elements of a market system. And Alum Rock teachers have been instrumental in preventing a competitive threat from a proposed new community school. An attempt to force the issue of competition could threaten the stability of the demonstration.

We can see from the above that only a voucher system that builds the competitive features into the basic program from the start is likely to benefit from the effects of the

Fig. 1. *Voucher used in Alum Rock, Calif., school district.*

market system. The Liberty plan recognizes this need and makes schools free and independent from the start. Free to be successful, and free to fail.

How did the students learn in the first year of the voucher demonstration? According to Albert Shanker, president of the American Federation of Teachers, the data indicate that the Alum Rock "panacea" is another washout. Shanker takes some of the test data showing a minor drop in achievement scores at the voucher schools and alleges that the failure is "devastating." Another Rand Corporation researcher, Pierce Barker, with a different set of tests, says that the "voucher demonstration had little or no effect, positive or negative, on academic achievement as measured." The Rand Corporation's director of the study, Daniel Weiler: "Mr. Shanker's characterization of our findings to date is not accurate, and should not be used as the basis for a judgment about the Alum Rock demonstration."

It is regrettable that one of education's leaders is so opposed to change that he twists the data. It may be that the voucher program is viewed as a threat to union leadership. It will be interesting to see how Mr. Shanker reacts to the Liberty plan's add-on tuition feature, which would provide jobs for many of his presently unemployed union members.

The state of New Hampshire, with Yankee tenacity, refused to be enticed into the "regulated voucher" scheme. The state's experimental program was originally planned to start in the fall of 1975. However, federal budget restrictions have sent it back to the planning stages. This is another example of education's addiction to federal money in order to get something done. As now planned, private, nonsectarian schools would be included. Provision was made for parochial schools to participate in the plan should their inclusion be ordered by the courts. If this is ordered, federal funds will cover tuition costs. Federal funds will also be used for incentive grants to participating school districts; for vouchers in private schools; added administrative costs; special transportation costs; and testing and evaluation.

Supplemental tuition may be provided by parents, should they wish to send their child to a school whose tuition is greater than the voucher. Parents will be free to use the voucher money in any "approved" school in the United States.

A similar federally financed voucher demonstration is planned for East Hartford, Connecticut. This district has had an open enrollment policy, of which the use of vouchers is an extension. As planned, private schools can be included but all schools are prohibited from charging additional tuition.

In *Public Schools of Choice*,[15] Mario Fantini shows how a voucher system can be operated within the existing public school system. In some way this is similar to what I propose as a temporary solution (Chapter 13), pending the enactment of enabling legislation for the Liberty School program.

Fantini proposes a system where each student is offered a classical academic prep school, a community-centered school, a school without walls, or other alternative, all within the public school operation. Although this type of plan purports to provide diversity and free choice, the packaging of diverse schools within a public school system is difficult to implement and maintain. As mentioned in connection with Alum Rock, competition is rejected by public school personnel. Since no schools are permitted outside the public system, parents' choices are narrowed. Fantini's requirement that all schools adhere to the same objectives reduces freedom to choose and implies that parents cannot be trusted to decide their own objectives.

3. Free Choice in Education through the Liberty Plan—Kindergarten through University

EDUCATION VOUCHERS ARE often thought of as something that would apply only to private and parochial schools. The Liberty plan envisages vouchers for all schools, including public schools, that freely wish to join the program. Nor would any startling or immediate changes come about. Schools would be free to evolve in response to the changing needs of students, parents, society, and to the developing art of education itself.

Nearly 92% of our elementary and secondary students are presently enrolled in public schools. So it would be folly to devise a system that would, with one stroke of the pen, sweep these away and attempt to substitute something completely new and untried.

Our objective with the Liberty plan should be to give the public schools a new environment in which they can thrive and grow, under the control of parents. To insure that the existing public schools have a head start, vouchers for nonpublic schools would be phased in over a five year period.

Governance

As nonprofit independent school associations, the formerly public schools would be controlled by parent-patrons through board members elected by them. These board members can be paid or voluntary in accordance with local custom.

Thus, control by parents will be double-barreled. They

will elect the school board governing the existing school district or system of schools, and they will have a choice of school districts, schools within the systems, and nonpublic schools outside the public sector. Freed of the territorial limitations inherited from their rural forebears, schools would be free to move competitively into other areas and to innovate program and curriculum.

For example, a school district in a fully developed area with declining enrollment would be able to seek students in an adjoining area where schools are crowded. The new area's school system might not find it necessary to construct additional schools and would be relieved of overcrowding. Taxpayers in the new area would not be overwhelmed by taxes to build new schools. Parents and students from the new area would find schools ready to receive them with enough space. The efficiency of the school system in the already developed area would increase as enrollment approached capacity.

The way we finance the construction and equipping of elementary and secondary public schools does not tend to make school managers conscious of and responsible for these costs. Educators must seek tax funds to build and equip buildings through bond issues supported by tax millage earmarked to pay off the bonds. Then they must ask the taxpayers for operating millage to permit them to operate the facility. Once bonds are sold and buildings are built and equipped, this investment is not presently considered by school management to be part of the operating cost. This is like building a factory to make widgets and then not including something in the price of the widgets to replace the factory when it wears out. HEW statistics for 1973 to 1974 indicate we spent nationally $1147.00 per pupil per year for operating costs, but in addition we spent 14% more, or $159.00, per pupil for buildings, land,

equipment and interest on the bonds issued to pay for them.

With the Liberty plan, funds for buildings and equipment would be included in one voucher, requiring attention of school management to this cost. Construction of new buildings could be handled by the sale of tax-free bonds, much as it is done now. Being obviously responsible for these funds, school management would tend to build functional schools rather than monuments.

The quality of education can only improve as school management becomes conscious of the refreshing competition from adjoining school districts and, in a few years, of the potential competition from nonpublic schools being phased into the system. The competitive climate need not exist for school districts alone but will reach down to the school level as districts see the need to decentralize authority in order to offer diverse programs.

Much of the public, particularly the poor, feel that massive school systems such as in Chicago, Detroit, New York, etc., have failed at their tasks because of excessive size and bureaucratic inertia. Responding to this situation, legislation should provide for individual schools or groups of schools to secede from the large system and operate independently. To insure against anarchy, rules should be set up requiring that a substantial majority of the parents involved wish to secede and that continuing management will be available.

Under the Liberty scheme, teacher certification, tenure and union relations would be the responsibility of the school systems, without state interference. As in private industry, state laws would neither require nor prohibit union membership. Union bargaining on a state or area-wide basis should be prohibited to insure the decentralized character of schools. At the same time, teachers should have the right to strike. The effect of these provisions would be to encourage school managements and employee groups to work together in pleasing parent customers (see Chapter 14).

Compared to public schools, private and parochial schools enroll only 8% of the students. But it will be important that they be included in the Liberty plan so that their students and parents not be treated as second class citizens. Further, the exclusion of religious schools would violate the guarantee of free exercise of religion provided by the First Amendment. Recent polls indicate that a majority of the public feel that states should contribute to the support of parochial schools.

Critics of voucher plans fear that there will be a proliferation of nonpublic schools of doubtful quality. They raise the specter of "hucksterism" and of private operators producing and marketing education like a can of beer. With any voucher plan, an explosive growth of nonpublic schools, whether operated by entrepreneurs or by nonprofit organizations, is not likely. Parents are cautious and conservative about the education of their children. Except for the most liberal among them, they will be slow to move their children to a new school. And it will be the forward-thinking few that will provide the pressure on school management to innovate and become more responsive.

We stated earlier that the Liberty plan would not cause any increased tax burden. To insure this, the voluntary entry of nonpublic schools into the system must be phased in to coincide with the decline in enrollment. For example, vouchers for the first year might be worth 20% of face value, 40% the second and 100% the fifth year. Thus, as enrollment declines in the public or independent schools, the per pupil expenditure can be kept the same for those 92 out of 100 students, while gradually increasing for those in nonpublic schools.

This method would not suddenly burden the public

with additional taxes and would give public schools a head start; a chance to get their house in order before being exposed to the full rigors of competition.

The Supreme Court of the United States has repeatedly rejected aid to religious schools on the constitutional grounds of being contrary to the first amendment (exercise and establishment of religion) and the fourteenth amendment (equal protection under laws). The common characteristic of these rejections was that aid was given to parents of parochial students *only* and not to parents of *all* children.

It would seem to this non-lawyer that the Liberty School system which provides vouchers of equal amount for all students would meet the requirements of the court, because it neither benefits nor imposes a burden on religion. Aid is given to all students equally and not to schools, whether religious or nonsectarian. Legal opinion confirms this view. Of interest is a legal brief prepared in the early 60's for the Department of Health, Education, and Welfare, entitled "The Impact of the First Amendment to the Constitution Upon Federal Aid to Education":

> The First Amendment does not require Government to be hostile to religion, nor does it permit governmental discrimination against religious activities. The objective is neutrality, however difficult it may be to be neutral or to determine what neutrality requires in relation to particular factual situations.

Of course, few people feel neutral about religion. The Liberty plan permits parents to do something or nothing about religious education for their children, as they see fit.

Add-on Tuition

One of the questions raised about nonpublic and parochial education might be "Some of these schools cost more than the public schools. How would the Liberty school system handle this?" In addition, some of the newly independent schools may have been spending more money than the state voucher and will elect to continue or increase this level of expenditure. Present laws regarding public schools effectively prohibit any charge to parents exceeding funds provided by taxes.

With the Liberty plan, schools may charge any amount they wish, in addition to the voucher. Of course, there will continue to be many schools operating within the amount of the state voucher and these schools will attract parents who do not wish to spend an extra amount. Competitive forces will maintain a balance between schools with and without add-in tuition.

Expensive schools will tend to attract better teachers because they can offer more money and better working conditions. Will the poorer schools be thus deprived? Actually, the reverse will be true. As in professional baseball, hundreds of aspiring players must first excel in the bush leagues, before only a few can be advanced to the big leagues. So with teachers; if they aspire to teach at a prestigious and well-paying school they must first prove their abilities in less expensive schools. Thus, many will be striving and, in the striving, teaching will improve. In the present situation, teachers are effectively prevented from demonstrating superior skill and hard work by peer group pressure and the fact that more money comes only from degrees and years of service. Even some of the poorer schools themselves will offer opportunity to aspiring teachers. Some schools will have master teachers, teachers with a large class size, specialty teachers, and there will be opportunities for teachers to become administrators.

But the economically disadvantaged, regardless of race, also need access to these higher cost schools. This can be provided by a requirement that any school charging an add-on must seek a 5% scholarship enrollment of the poor, regardless of race. The additional funds going into schools because of this add-on feature should substantially reduce the ranks of unemployed teachers.

Schools of Last Resort?

We have discussed freedom for parents and students to choose a school suitable for their learning style and we will later discuss how teachers should be free to choose a school compatible with their teaching philosophy. The concurrent freedom must be the right of schools to select a student body with a learning style suitable for the program offered.

If we allow schools to choose among applicants, are we in danger of some schools becoming "schools of last resort" or dumping grounds for slow or disruptive students? Will some students find no school at all willing to receive them? Since most of the problem students result from their not having a school corresponding to their learning style, the free choice principle will insure that almost every student will be welcomed in some school. Of the remaining few, some have learning disabilities entitling them to extra vouchers. These extra vouchers will make them attractive to special schools organized for this purpose. Another tiny group can be classed as juvenile delinquents. These are a problem for the courts, not schools. Even a few delinquent students can destroy the learning environment of a thousand students. This is one of the major problems in schools today.

With this facet of the Liberty plan, we must remember that surplus spaces in schools resulting from falling enrollment will make for a buyers' market in schools. Administrators will seek voucher-bearing students, and work to retain them. And this will not be a passing situation, but will remain true for many years to come.

Discrimination

With this feature of the Liberty plan, how would discrimination be prevented? Critics will say that a determined school management will find ways to discriminate. Of course, they are right. Subtle standards can be used to rule out the unwanted, such as "academic ability," "lack of talent" or simply "incompatibility." The spaces for the poor can be filled by the children of widows, children of clergymen or others of the same means and social class, who may qualify as poor.

But these statements ignore several facts about the present population, and its social consciousness. For the first time in our history we have a surplus of everything available to schools. We have surplus desks, surplus classrooms, surplus buildings and surplus teachers. Everything is surplus except students. This supply-demand situation, if it is given the opportunity, will work against discrimination in school enrollment. Segregationist tendencies will be overwhelmed by economics—the demand for voucher-bearing students.

Second, there is increasing realization that schools with a multi-cultural and/or multi-ethnic student body have much to contribute to our society and the individual student. Given this fact, a little time to adjust, and free choice of schools, the discrimination bugaboo is going to fade into history. The trouble comes when governmental bodies or courts attempt to achieve integration by force.

Finally, we must realize that the Liberty plan's potential for improving schools for students of all races and all economic classes is so great that it would be the height of folly to regulate it to death at the outset. It is possible to design bureaucratic agencies which would attempt to prevent segregation. But in the process these agencies will destroy the very freedom that the Liberty plan depends upon for success. In order to enjoy our high standard of living, we are willing to accept defects in automobiles, houses, in everything we buy. So with schools. If we are going to vastly improve schools with the principles of Liberty, we cannot expect perfection in the elimination of discrimination at the outset.

Despite the above, there are going to be some schools whose management or clientele will reject integration. How can we discourage this? Implementing state legislation can specify that selection of both the regular and scholarship students be "blind." Data files going to the school's selection board would have no mention of race, or economic class. Despite penalties which may be provided, even this procedure can be circumvented; however, the present situation far exceeds the amount of discrimination that would slip by under the Liberty plan.

The final safeguard would be judicial. For example, if 20% of applicants were minorities and none or only a token few were accepted, then proof would exist of discrimination. Complaining parents could collect damages and the school's vouchers could be reduced in value. In flagrant cases, the school could be excluded from the Liberty system, and its vouchers cut off.

Sponsors of forced busing to effect racial integration are related to those friendly folk who brought us prohibition and the automobile seat-belt interlock system and, in the end, will probably have as much success. But polls confirm that the rest of us, while we believe that racial integration is a desirable social objective, are opposed to force. Of those in favor of integration, only a minority of both whites and blacks think forced busing is the best way to achieve it (Gallup Poll).[4]

Transportation Requirements

The Liberty plan would encourage integration by providing access for racial and other minorities to any school of their choice, even the most expensive. Any qualified student can attend any school in the state. But to make this a practical reality, transportation must be available.

An organization called the Liberty School Sector would be formed to insure the availability of transportation within its areas, together with other duties now performed by the state or intermediate school districts. The Sector would be composed of around 200,000 pupils with a roughly representative racial and income level makeup. Schematically, it would be like a slice of pie, with lower income families at one end, upper income at the other and middle income in between. Actually, the sector could be any shape and some parts might not even be contiguous. (See Figure 2.)

Influencing the size and the shape of the sector would be the availability of urban transportation such as subways, commuter trains, and expressways. In some areas, a grid of shuttle buses, east-west and north-south, will prove effective with stops and transfer points at schools. (See Chapter 4 for in-depth discussion.)

The Liberty School Sector will be an important organization in providing free choice of schools. We will look at what its duties and responsibility would be in the next chapters, as well as how it would handle the transportation necessary to make free choice into reality.

Higher Education

The inequity in the way we distribute tax money for higher education is shocking. The middle class is taxed

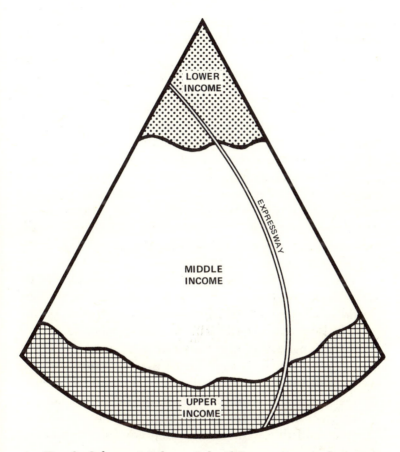

Fig. 2. Schematic Liberty School Sector. In actual practice, the sector could be any shape. It should include an income and racially representative student population. The idea would be to provide practical opportunities for any student to attend any school in the sector.

to provide the best schools for the rich and the poor. Smaller private colleges and universities are dying out because they cannot compete with state-supported schools. Yet these state-supported institutions are most inefficient and cost students and taxpayers as much as three times the equivalent educational services purchased from an efficient privately run school.

Nationwide, a year at publicly controlled institution of higher education costs taxpayers on the average $3600.00, plus $500.00 of tuition from the student. This is in addition to room and board. (HEW's Statistics for 1973-74).[5] The taxpayer is not given the opportunity to take his portion of the $3600.00 to an institution of his choice. Should you decide to attend a nonpublic college in your state or a public or nonpublic school in another state, then you must pay your own way while paying taxes to support others who attend your state's schools. This $4100.00 is nearly enough to pay the entire four year tuition at some small, efficient nonpublic colleges.

The Liberty Plan for higher education would give the tax money to the student, rather than the institution. Students would be able to attend any approved institution, public, private, religious, vocational and even foreign schools. A statistical analysis of the amounts we spend on higher education and the numbers who use these education services would indicate that we can give every individual reaching 18 years of age an entitlement of $14,000.00 to be used at any institution of his or her choice at any time in his lifetime. And this without spending any more tax money than we do now!

Much as we do with high cost elementary and secondary schools, expensive heavily endowed universities electing to join the Liberty plan would be required to provide scholarships for the poor. This could be related to the amount of their income from gifts and endowments. Details of the operation of the Liberty plan for higher education are in Chapter 15.

4. The Liberty School Sector—Supervision—Buildings—Equipment and Transportation

WE HAVE DISCUSSED the need for diversity in education in order to better serve students with differing learning styles. The Liberty School plan has been presented as the way to provide this freedom of choice. In theory, parents can send their children to any Liberty School in the state. In practice, the choice would be limited to schools within a reasonable distance of the student's home, depending on available transportation. Therefore, unless we make the choice effective by providing a way for students to reach the chosen school, the idea will be only so much rhetoric.

This objective can be accomplished if we take a slice of the metropolitan or other area having a representative income and racial population and call it the Liberty School Sector. As stated, earlier, the sector could have a pupil population of around 200,000. Schematically, it might be like a piece of pie, with lower income families at one end, upper income at the other and middle income between. Geography and population distribution may dictate completely different shapes and some parts might not even be connected. The size and shape of the Sector would also be affected by the availability of public transportation, expressways, etc. Boundaries of the sector may not be parallel with the constituent school districts' boundaries, but could bisect them as other factors may indicate.

Although the Sector's most important task would be the provision of transportation and its physical layout would be designed to assist in this task, it would also be a convenient administrative unit to handle minimum supervisory duties and provide services now handled by intermediate school districts and state departments of education. Among its duties could be: the distribution of vouchers; certification of vouchers returned by schools for cash; provision of extra vouchers for the retarded and others with learning disabilities; administration of achievement or other tests; counseling services to advise parents on available schools; disposal of surplus buildings and equipment; and provision of a backup guarantee on bonds issued for new buildings. To insure that the Sector does not become another bureaucratic colossus or interfere with the autonomy of individual schools or districts, its authority should be clearly limited in the enabling legislation.

If schools are burdened by unnecessary regulation, they will be unable to respond in a free market manner to the needs of their parent patrons. One of the ways that we can insure this limited control would be to have the Liberty School Sector's controlling board elected by the constituent schools.

Transportation

Few parents have the time or the money for expensive gasoline to drive their children to the chosen school, however superior it may be. Even car pools would only provide a partial solution, and that only for affluent two-car families in the suburbs. Public transportation, where available, can effectively transport secondary students, but elementary students may not be able to cope with this type of movement.

At the present time, big city school districts provide little, if any, school bus transportation. The density of population has caused most schools to be located so that students can walk to schools of all grade levels. Transportation to specialized vocational schools requires the student to pay for transportation on public buses or subways. Frequently, specially priced tickets are provided, with free tickets for the poor. Special-education students can be handled by mini-buses or by contractual arrangements with local taxi companies, as in Detroit.

In the suburbs, many of the elementary schools are located within walking distance of their patrons, although in sparsely settled areas children living over one or one and a half miles away are provided bus transportation. Secondary schools are frequently located beyond walking distance, and bus transportation is offered. Buses make several runs per day, picking up students at or near their homes. This transportation is inefficient in that buses travel with one-way loads only.

A transportation plan should minimize the use of scarce fuel. At present, transportation for after-school activities is handled by parents or, in the more affluent areas where families have a spare car, by students themselves. In warmer seasons, bicycles are frequently used. Here are some of the ways transportation can be provided under the Liberty plan:

(1) Where a good network of public transportation is available, it can be used almost exclusively.

(2) Public transportation and school buses can be used in a coordinated manner.

(3) School buses may be used exclusively. See Figure 3. Under this arrangement, elementary children get to their local schools just as they do now, by walking or by bus. Secondary youngsters walk to the nearest school, of any description. If the secondary school is simply too far, the students can ride the same bus as elementary children to their neighborhood

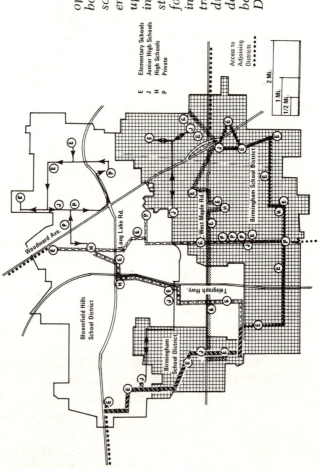

Fig. 3. Shuttle buses operate continuously in both directions when schools are starting or ending the day. Buses pick up students while traveling in both directions, stopping only at schools for safety. Where routes intersect students can transfer to buses going in different directions. Plan developed for two suburban school districts near Detroit.

E   Elementary Schools
J   Junior High Schools
H   High Schools
P   Private

•••••   Access to
        Adjoining
        Districts

2 Mi.
1 Mi.
1/2 Mi.

Woodward Ave.

Long Lake Rd.

Bloomfield Hills
School District

E. West Maple Rd.

Telegraph Hwy.

Birmingham
School District

Birmingham School District

elementary schools and continue from there. Shuttle buses, operating continuously when schools are starting or ending the day, cut across the area, stopping at all schools. Maximum efficiency is attained, because the buses pick up students while traveling in both directions. Where routes intersect, students can transfer to buses going in different directions. Urban or school bus transportation coming from other areas in the LSS can feed into this minisystem.

These shuttle buses should operate for several hours after school hours to provide rides for students involved in athletic practice, drama, enrichment programs and all of the myriad after-school activities.

This system provides maximum safety for children because they board buses at schools only, not on busy highways. At the same time it would cost less than the present bus operation.

(4) The Grid system. School buses operate a shuttle service on mile roads, north-south and east-west. Children are picked up on demand at specified points. This method is in use in the Denver, Colorado, area.

The cost of operating the sector's transportation system should be spread against all schools in the sector. Were it to be otherwise, the selection of scholarship students by expensive schools might be affected by transportation costs. Further, the available transportation benefits all of the students in the sector by improving schools through free market competition.

Some students, particularly those living along the boundary of an adjoining Sector, may wish to attend a school outside their home Sector. They should be free to do so. To facilitate this, interchange points should be provided for adjoining transportation systems. This feature would broaden the available choices.

Buildings and Equipment

In addition to transportation, another important responsibility of the Liberty School Sector would be buildings and equipment. This would include transfer of these properties to the newly formed independent school systems, disposal of surplus property, and assistance to new or growing schools in providing financing for real estate, buildings and equipment.

The equipment, buildings and real estate of existing school systems have been paid for by taxpayers of either the state or the local school district, usually both. In addition, much debt is outstanding in the form of long-term bonds. If the now independent school systems were to become owners of this property and assume the outstanding debt in connection, many inequities would result. Some school districts would receive a windfall in the form of paid-up equipment, buildings and real estate, while others would be saddled with a huge debt. Another way to look at it: school systems should be constrained to use only the equipment and property they really need. Otherwise some systems would be badly in need of new or used buildings and equipment, but would have no funds to purchase them.

The Liberty plan would have the state, through the Liberty School Sector, assume title to all public school property. The newly independent schools would then select those buildings and equipment that they are occupying and wished to retain, purchasing them from the sector. Price would be based on appraised value and remaining useful life. Outstanding bonds would then be assumed by the state. Terms can be adjusted realistically to permit pay-off, with interest, at an annual rate well within the school system's budget.

The voucher amount would be adjusted so that, state-wide, schools could purchase all buildings and equipment they wished to retain and schools in developing areas or new schools would have funds to purchase the property they used, without an increase in taxes.

Statewide, the average voucher for all grade levels would be the same as is being now spent on schools by the state, federal and local governments, divided by the number of pupils. For example, nationally, this figure in the 73-74 school year was $1306.00 (HEW figures). Of this amount, $159.00 was the spending for capital investment, including interest costs. Of course, different grade levels would have vouchers of different values, since it costs more to build and operate secondary schools than elementary schools.

The $1306.00 per year, adjusted for today's higher costs, would be the average nationwide voucher per pupil. In some states, the voucher amount would be higher, some lower. It is not the intent to earmark 14% or $159.00 for buildings, equipment and interest. School managers would be free to allocate the total voucher as indicated by their efficiency and by the demands of the parent customers.

For example, our average school is spending $1147.00 per year for operating costs and $159.00 for capital costs, and upon becoming an independent school would receive a voucher for $1306.00 (average) for each student. We can assume on the same average basis that the Liberty sector would then sell this property to the school for a price based on the valuation and remaining useful life and then the annual payments on this debt would average $159.00 per pupil per year. As part of the transaction, the Sector would assume the obligation of whatever outstanding indebtedness existed in connection with this property. In this example, the schools' present and future costs would represent a wash sale, or no change in expense or income. But we are not just juggling figures. We are giving school managers broader options in the way they allocate their money.

But the example given above is for a national average school system. How about one with a surplus of schools? The system might decide to purchase from the Sector land, buildings, and equipment on which their annual payments would be only $100.00 per pupil. School management would be free to spend the $59.00 on improving the instructional program. The Liberty sector would offer to sell the surplus buildings and equipment first to other school systems and then on the open market. Either way, there would be no increased cost to the taxpayer or the schools. At the same time, surplus equipment, and sometimes buildings, could be recycled into school systems with an increasing student body.

5. Secondary Schools—14 and Out?—Vocational Schools

"The nation does not need laws that force adolescents to go to school. It needs schools and school related programs that make adolescents wish to come." [Report of the National Commission on the Reform of Secondary Education[6]]

THE NATIONAL COMMISSION'S conclusions suggest many reasons why we need diversity and choice in secondary schools. Their findings on earlier maturity:

Today's schools must come to terms with the earlier maturation of students, both sexual and physical. The mean age at which girls reach menarche seems to have been declining steadily for at least a century. Voice change in boys which occurred at an average age of eighteen in the eighteenth century, is now occurring at an average age of 13.3 years. . . . Correlations have been reported between increased stature and higher mental scores . . . [with] wide social and educational implications; schools cannot ignore them.

On enrollment decline: " . . . secondary schools will experience a drop of more than two million in student enrollment between 1973 and 1984. . . . It is hard to believe that taxpayers are going to pay as much for smaller schools as they did for larger ones.

"Even steeper declines in the enrollment of the comprehensive high school may result from the reforms this Commission proposes."

On compulsory attendance: "The formal school leaving

age should be dropped to age fourteen. Other programs should accomodate those who wish to leave school, and employment laws should be rewritten to assure on-the-job training in full time service and work.

"The harm done to the school by the student who does not want to be there is measured not only by the incidence of vandalism and assault but also by a subtle and continuous degradation of the tone of the educational enterprise."

Much of today's violence in schools stems from a rebellion of the students *compelled* to be there. They are compelled to attend by law and by a school establishment that does not recognize their maturity or intellectual competence. The curriculum is aimed at the least common denominator among them. As a result, the vast majority find programs offered childish and a waste of their time. Teachers think of themselves as jailers and students consider themselves inmates. The resulting environment is neither a satisfactory teaching nor learning situation. Some students are able to mesmerize themselves into accepting this lack of challenge and stimulation. Others rebel and make of the school an arena of violence where administrators and teachers pit their ability to control against the students' ability to disrupt.

As an essential part of the above recommendation, the commission urges alternative types of education for the school-leaving youth. At least as much school money should be available to them for programs such as on-the-job training as would have been spent had they remained in school. The establishment of an organization like the Civilian Conservation Corps (CCC) of the '30s to provide an outlet for youngsters leaving school is suggested.

Another recommendation: " . . . entitle each citizen to fourteen years of tuition free education beyond kindergarten, only eight of which would be compulsory. The remaining six years would be available for use by anyone at any stage of his life."

The Liberty plan agrees with this recommendation but would limit the child's entitlement in terms of years to kindergarten plus twelve. In addition a dollar sum would be provided for college or higher education (See Chapter 15.)

Some students complete the K-12 program in less than the 13 years normally required. We should investigate the desirability of rewarding this ability and hard work by adding the unused voucher credits to their higher education entitlement.

For high school dropouts who wish to resume their education and who have had learning experiences or individual study since leaving school, we should provide examinations on the level of a School Level Examination Program (SLEP) to provide credit for learning attained outside schools.

Diversity and free choice in high schools will cause them to create and offer classes not offered by other schools, thus proliferating the choices available to students. Exciting programs like Philadelphia's Parkway Program, with students learning in "on the town," and work-study programs, can be offered.

Some of the high schools can be on a year-round calendar. Along with the 45/15 they might consider the Four Quarter, Quinmester, and Concept 6 with 4, 5 and 6 school periods annually. Options should be presented for part-time employment, early graduation, choice of vacation season, or no vacation at all.

Critics may say that the reduction in the school-leaving age will flood the market with teen-agers seeking employment. The reverse could well be true. The teen-age population, like the school population, will be declining rapidly so that those leaving school should find ample employment opportunity in jobs normally filled by youngsters.

The benefits accruing to high school students, their parents and the community as a whole are overwhelming reasons for freedom of choice in schools.

Good vocational schools have classes on three shifts, year-round, while other high schools face absenteeism and declining enrollment. Why are discipline, vandalism and attendance problems minimal in vocational schools while escalating in traditional schools?

The difference lies in the fact that students want to attend. They are not forced to go. The lesson here is the same as the recommendation of the Commission cited at the opening of this chapter: "The nation does not need laws that force adolescents to go to school. It needs schools and school related programs that make adolescents wish to come."

Allen Matheson, director of an Oakland County, Michigan, public vocational school, quotes his students as saying that the school "turns them on to study and learning." While most of the students choose the part-time vocational school because they do not intend to go on to college, some change their minds after the vocational school experience. Job placement of graduates is 95%, including those who decide to go to college.

But vocational schools cost more money than regular high schools. How could funds be provided without an increase in taxes?

The answer may lie in the fact that vocational schools tend to increase the student's lifetime earning power, as does higher education in general. We should consider permitting the student to draw down a portion of his higher education entitlement to be added to his secondary school voucher. The combination of the two would be enough to cover the cost of the secondary level vocational school.

6. Moral Education—Religious Schools—Private Schools

PRIVATE AND PAROCHIAL schools, including elementary, secondary and vocational schools, are an important part of our American school system. Although they presently account for only 8% of the enrollment, they provide attractive alternatives to the public schools. Once they become a part of the Liberty plan and are assimilated into it, they will be in a position to continue and expand their role.

Practical, economy-minded citizens may well pose the question: "Why should private and religious schools be included in the Liberty plan?" It can be said that private schools are mainly patronized by the rich, and their patrons will probably continue to send their children to these expensive schools without the benefit of the tax-provided Liberty voucher. Some can also say that parents who presently send their children to religious schools are determined to do so with or without help from the taxpayers in the form of vouchers. It would seem to follow that provision of public funds for these schools through the Liberty vouchers would be a burden on taxpayers that would make no improvement in schools, simply cost more! But the reasons for including private and religious schools are substantial.

Equity demands that if we provide vouchers for the 92% of students presently enrolled in public schools, then both legally and morally we would have no valid reason for not providing the same for the 8% enrolled in private and religious schools. Earlier plans to provide assistance to parents of nonpublic school students have been struck down in the courts because they assisted one class but not the other. That is, vouchers or tax credits were to be given parents of nonpublic school children but not to parents of public school children. Therefore, it would seem that the courts would treat the *exclusion* of private and parochial school students in a like manner. The exclusion of one class of students may place the entire idea in jeopardy.

We need pluralism and diversity in our schools. Since the present public schools are largely homogenous and some may remain that way after the Liberty plan is implemented, the present nonpublic schools will aid in offering the diversity essential for progress. It is a mistake to assume that the decline in the number of nonpublic schools has been arrested. The reduction in their numbers exceeds that caused by falling enrollment and is due largely to escalating tuition costs. Further, since the nonpublic schools in some areas may have been the only source of this student-oriented freedom of choice, and a central attribute of the Liberty plan is the provision of different types of schools to satisfy different student learning styles, their inclusion is logical.

Another important reason for vouchers for these schools is the leverage they will provide for the poor and minorities. The 5% scholarship requirement for schools spending more than the state voucher will provide access to these schools for those who cannot afford it, and will aid both racial integration and upward social mobility.

Watergate may have been the straw that broke the camel's back in terms of moral frustration, but ethical problems from shoplifting to drug abuse to rising crime rates in general have long given parents reason to be enthusiastic over education on right and wrong for our future citizens. Despite the permission of optional religious education and/or value clarification in the independent Liberty schools, a variety of religious schools—Catholic, Protestant, Jewish and others—will be of vast benefit to the future of our society.

Our refusal of tax support for religious schools penalizes parents who wish to give their children a value system which differs from the consensus values of the community. No matter how hard we try not to, schools do tend to teach the value system of the majority. These values are then modified by still another set of values—of those making the delivery, the teachers.

There is, then, a need for private and religious schools as a part of the Liberty plan. Now let us look further into the need for *moral education.*

A survey by the *Christian Science Monitor* found substantial parental enthusiasm for courses in "moral development," "character education" and "value clarification." In the old days of the 3R's, schools and school books sought to impart an ethical consciousness. But as our society became more pluralistic, state-run schools came into conflict with personal and private beliefs in their efforts to instill ethical and moral principles. The reaction has been to avoid confrontation and to teach less and less in this important area. Court decisions have expedited this trend.

Let us hope that the moral revival that the *Monitor* sees will at least encourage instruction in timeless principles like "do unto others as you would have them do unto you."

The interests of our society and national survival demand a renaissance in ethical teaching and beliefs. Some would have us believe that what we should teach about honesty, stealing and respect for our fellow man is constantly changing. This cannot be so. The dissolution of empires and civilizations in the past has been preceded by a deterioration in these beliefs. As George Washington, our first President, said in his farewell address:

Of all the dispositions and habits which lead to political prosperity, religion and morality are indispensable supports. In vain would that man claim the tribute of patriotism who should labor to subvert these great pillars of human happiness—these firmest props of the duties of men and citizens.

The very organization of our public schools, with prohibition of religious instruction, and the reluctance to even teach *about* it, is immoral. We require that parents and students surrender their freedom of religion as a condition for sharing in the state's educational funds. There must be other ways than state-controlled schools teaching secular humanism to insure the freedom of religion guaranteed by our constitution.

In *Things to Come* by Herman Kahn and B. Bruce-Biggs the authors recognize the strong possibility of a religious education counterreformation:

> Protestant parochial schools are a possibility. So long as the U.S. public schools were essentially Protestant schools (which is why the Roman Catholics felt the need to operate a parallel school system), church-related Protestant sectarian education was unnecessary. But today, an orthodox Protestant Christian (not to mention a Fundamentalist) can make a good case that, from his point of view, the public schools are proselytizing secular humanism and its explicitly anti-Christian values. Thanks to the U.S. Supreme Court, children at public schools are not even permitted to pray; and they are taught 'value-free' sex education. . . . If these counter culture tendencies in the schools continue, as some of the best young educators want them to, the public schools will become 'corrupt' and 'immoral' institutions that no 'decent' Christian would want his children to attend.

A recent Gallup Poll of Public Attitudes Toward Education reveals that 77% of the people would support a constitutional amendment to permit prayers to be said in public schools. Yet the framers of the Constitution and the Bill of Rights correctly anticipated the danger to both religious and secular freedom that would result from even this potential change. So it seems clear to many that the Supreme Court in its opinions about the Separation of Church and State has been consistent with the spirit and intent of the Founding Fathers.

Yet the need for instruction in moral principles exists. The revitalized, vigorous independent public schools under the Liberty plan will be legally able to fill this need. Such instruction may be theology-based, humanist, or, at the option of parents, be omitted entirely from their youngster's curriculum. Responding to the religious affiliations of the student body, clergy from any number of faiths may offer voluntary classes in these formerly public schools. In addition, parents would be free to choose a religious school, giving them the maximum freedom of choice.

Because thousands of parochial school classrooms have been closed, thus exacerabating the financial difficulties of public schools, a number of states have tried to find ways to help keep religious schools open. Whether prompted by expediency or conviction, public support for nonpublic schools is not a new idea and is endorsed by a majority of the people. We have long recognized that important goals of the public as a whole can be achieved through church-sponsored schools.

Every state, and in some cases the Federal Government, has provided assistance for children attending qualified religious schools. This assistance has been in the fringe areas such as transportation, health services, enriched dietary programs, provisions for the handicapped, textbooks and driver education. The nature of this aid is that it helps the child and not the school.

When it came to the operation of school buses, the

Supreme Court said that the exclusion of students of parochial schools from the bus service was an imposed burden on the free exercise of religion. Some responded also that the failure of the government to provide aid to private or parochial schools is in itself an anti-religious act because parents will be subject to financial pressures caused by at once paying taxes to support public schools and tuition for their religious schools, thus encouraging them to violate their religious beliefs by sending their children to nonreligious schools. But what the Supreme Court has said is that it will not tolerate either governmentally established religion or governmental interference with religion.

It would seem to this nonlawyer that the Liberty system which provides vouchers of equal amount for all students would meet the requirements of the court, because it neither benefits nor imposes a burden on religion. On the other hand, a voucher system, like New Hampshire's planned experiment, in which only nonreligious schools participate initially, would unnecessarily impose a burden on religion contrary to the Constitution.

An article in the University of Michigan's Law Review[8] explores this question:

> Any aid to religious functions is suspect because it tends to encourage religion. However, if the aid is given to religious interests merely as part of a program aiding a broader class of beneficiaries, the problem of encouragement should be ameliorated by the fact that a denial of aid to religious interests alone would tend to inhibit religion.
>
> * * *
>
> A full voucher system will be able to avoid the special treatment pitfall if the monetary value of

the voucher is high enough. If it is, parents who do not belong to a religious denomination that already supports a system of sectarian schools may want to use the vouchers at nonsectarian private schools and, in response to this demand, many new private schools may be able to come into existence. In that case, the state voucher system would not benefit a predominantly religious class but would offer realistic private educational alternatives to all its citizens.

Religious schools under the Liberty plan would not, except for the sponsorship of a religious body, and their religious instruction, have any different characteristics than the independent and formerly public schools. They would be required to have the same basic curriculum and to achieve the minimum instructional objectives set forth for all schools.

But questions will be raised about restrictions imposed by church-related schools on the religious affiliation of their students. There may be reasons why non-church members may wish to send their children to a church-related school. Among these would be the proximity of the school to the student's home and the quality of the school's program. Nevertheless, religious schools should be able to give priority to members of their own religion, without other discrimination such as race or economic class.

Once nonmembers are admitted, can they be required to attend religious education classes and participate in religious ceremonies? The answer must be "no," because otherwise the schools might be guilty of religious discrimination, prohibited in Liberty schools. For instance, the Black Muslim schools are reported to be excellent schools but with an anti-white bias. These schools would qualify under the Liberty plan if their admission rules do not discriminate against white, Christian or other religious enrollment.

But religious schools should have the right to select their nonmember enrollment from among the applicants on a nondiscrimatory basis, as we suggest in connection with private schools. With the present and future birth dearth, this is likely to be a nonproblem, as schools of all types will be seeking voucher-bearing students.

There is no clear-cut difference between religious and private schools. Some private schools have nonsectarian religious instruction and ceremonies. So it is not easy to categorize them, except that they are usually not officially connected with a religious group.

Like all other Liberty schools, independent and church-related, private schools would be required to provide scholarships equal in number to 5% of their enrollment if their tuition exceeds the state provided voucher. This scholarship group would come from those unable to afford the add-on tuition, regardless of race.

Many private schools have long recognized the difference between students and some schools plan their program for students with fairly well-defined learning styles. Unlike the "Regulated" voucher plan developed by the Center for the Study of Public Policy (Chapter 2), which bases student selection partly on a lottery among the applicants, the Liberty plan would permit the school to select from among the scholarship applicants those it feels would be compatible with the program.

The economics are such that some schools would find it to their advantage to have much more than 5% scholarships. For example, if a school is staffed and equipped for 1000 pupils but enrolls only 900 with an add-on of $400.00, legislation would require 45 scholarship students. Should school management elect to have 100 or 55 extra scholarships and the statewide voucher is $1200.00, then the school would gain 55 × $1200 or $66,000 of additional income. This is money they would not otherwise have, and the cost to handle the additional students would be little or nothing. The public as a whole would benefit by receiving the add-on in the educational system without it coming from taxpayers. This is what we mean by leverage. This example may be the rule in schools for years to come as the low birth rate works its way through the grades. Scholarships in boarding schools would necessarily include the cost of board and room. Likewise, uniforms should be included for military schools.

Earlier we discussed how the voucher for nonpublic schools would be phased in over a period of five years. The voucher would be worth 20% the first year, 40% the second and 100% the fifth year. This provision would tend to keep the cost of schools level insofar as the taxpayers are concerned, because the enrollment decline would parallel the gradual addition of nonpublic schools to the voucher system. At the same time, the per pupil expenditure can be kept the same.

Another advantage this "phasing-in" would have: There would be no need to handle the nonpublic school buildings and equipment as was discussed for public schools in Chapter 4, with the Sector taking title and selling them back to the newly independent schools. This feature would probably eliminate a sticky legal problem about the equity between public and nonpublic schools.

In discussing the public schools, we proposed that they should be controlled by boards elected by the using parents. How should private and church-related schools be controlled? Some will urge that when these schools join the Liberty system, they be subject to this same rule. Many parents of parochial and private school children resent the control of schools by church hierarchies or by self-perpetuating boards of trustees. They feel that they should have more participation in the direction of schools, other than the typical PTA.

But consider the impact of parent control of religious schools. In church-related schools, wouldn't it be a rule affecting the "establishment of religion"? The combination of parents' freedom to choose schools and the buyer's market caused by declining enrollment is going to make these schools infinitely more responsive. As part of this new responsiveness, many well-run private and religious schools will probably change their administrative structure.

Private schools have developed over many years a very effective and continuing procedure for governance. Board membership may include alumni, trustees or executors of donors, parents, faculty, etc. Finally, regulation of this type may eliminate some schools that would otherwise become part of the Liberty program and would accomplish little for the quality of education, merely inflate the administrative bureaucracy. In the end, the best control that parents will have is that, with voucher in hand, they may move to a school controlled in accord with their beliefs.

In order to start a new school, an organization or a proprietor would simply have to show the state that competent, continuing management, financial resources and interested parents are all available. New schools should be encouraged so we may have the diversity and competition essential to improving all schools. New small schools should be able to purchase specialized services from the larger independent or private schools, or organizations especially formed for the purpose.

Next, we should take a look at the role of governments in education; how they got into the act; what they do now; and what the role of governments would be under the Liberty plan.

7. The Government in Education

THE DANGERS OF state-controlled education are evident to those who care to look at pre-World War II education in Germany, Italy and Japan. Add to that list all totalitarian countries of today including Russia, Cuba, China and the other nations behind the Iron Curtain. Control of the schools is essential for continuing totalitarian control of governments whether they be communist or fascist. The imposition of totalitarian forms of government on a nation whose young has been educated in the environment of freedom in Liberty Schools would be accomplished only with total military occupation.

Taking the government out of education is treated here primarily as a practical matter having to do with education alone, without reference to the pros and cons of the philosophy of big government. But let us make a small detour and consider the performance of our governments as a reference point to the efficiency that can be expected of government in education.

Consider the utter failure of government in public housing. Think of the Post Office. How about the railroads and their ills caused by excessive governmental regulation? If you have served in the Armed Forces, remember the waste and inefficiency with which we wage war. The track record is not good.

We consider our nation's economic system as being founded on free enterprise. Despite the many erosions inflicted on this system by increasing government control, it remains by far the most productive in the world. Why, then, the anomaly of government control over education, which controls the productive lives of nearly one third of the population? Surely the way we operate schools is socialistic. When we add this one third of the population to other operations of government which can be termed socialistic, it is difficult to say that we are still in a private enterprise economy.

Yet there is an opportunity to move this one third from socialistic control to individual free choice, and achieve a massive and exhilarating increase in personal freedoms.

The Liberty School plan requires that government supervision of schools be held to a practical minimum. The task of States would be the provision of funds for vouchers with the fewest possible strings attached. Schools are now controlled by a combination of local school boards, state legislatures and bureaucracies and, increasingly, by the Federal Congress and bureaucracy. The Liberty plan envisages schools controlled largely by parents. The limitations on government control should be based on the principle of a narrowly defined public purpose.

Historical Background

A discussion of the public purpose in education should be preceded by a bit of historical background. Martin Luther in 1524 urged the German state to establish compulsory public schools. His reasoning to the rulers was that universal, compulsory education would make the young men into better military material, while instructing them in their religion, thus giving the state a greater war potential and suppressing religious dissent.

In the same century, another religious reformer, John Calvin, established compulsory schools in Geneva with similar objectives. Under the Calvin influence, Holland established compulsory public schools in the early 1600's. Since the Puritans in the Massachusetts Bay Colony were

Calvinists from Holland, it is no surprise that they instituted compulsory schools in America.

After the American revolution, compulsory schooling spread to the other colonies and at the same time the specious theory that the children belonged to the government and not to their parents began to take shape as another reason for compulsory education.

In the early 1800's, as immigration began to accelerate, education was looked at as a way to homogenize these strange Irish, Germans, etc., fitting them into the mold of Protestant America. The Irish Catholics were to be "Christianized," which means "Protestantized." Hence the development of the Catholic parochial schools. Educationist Horace Mann wanted to "inform and regulate the will of the people." He also wanted to assimilate the lower classes and prevent civil strife through education. By the end of the century, compulsory public education was required in every state in the Union and the system of schools in cities was controlled by a heavy-handed bureaucracy, with uniform rules and standardized curriculum.

The late 1800's saw the full development of the one-room rural school house, serving, typically, a township or an area of six miles on a side or 36 square miles. If the school was located in the center of this square, then no pupil would have to walk more than three or four miles to school.

Since the United States was then 90% agrarian, this was probably the type of school attended by our ancestors. Under the state bureaucracy, control was vested in a locally elected board of education and financed through local taxes. Unless you were among the very few wealthy who could afford to send their children to distant boarding schools, there was no real alternative to compulsory education in the public schools. From this school system has descended, after mergers and consolidations, our present day system.

The circumstances favoring diversity and choice were non-existent in those days.

In Oregon, in a 1922 law, those in favor of total and universal compulsory education attempted to outlaw all private and church-related schools, even when they were state certified. The law would have compelled all children to attend public school, stamping out all choice in education. The Ku Klux Klan vigorously supported this law, hoping to eliminate the Catholic schools and to act for the "preservation of free institutions." In 1925, the Supreme Court struck down this attempt (Pierce vs. Society of Sisters). The court ruled that "the child is not the mere creature of the state" and determined that the law violated "the fundamental theory of liberty upon which all governments in this Union repose."

Let's go back now to the original purpose of compulsory public education: molding future soldiers and insuring against religious dissent. In terms of military need, fighting in lines or phalanxes without any individual initiative was how wars were fought. War occurred frequently, requiring nations to marshal all their resources or perish. Today, although our military still instructs in close order drill for "discipline" and for parades, actual wars are fought with primary reliance on individual initiative. We no longer need compulsory education in order to provide raw material for the armed forces. Insofar as religious uniformity goes, as discussed in the last chapter, we today avoid teaching about religion altogether, eliminating the second element of compulsory education's original purpose.

Our uniform schools did have some value in our industrial era, as they disciplined the young to do production-line jobs. At the same time they taught the children of the lower classes to keep their place, subservient to the managers in the hierarchy over them. But now we are entering what is called the "post-industrial" phase of our development, which demands variety in schooling, stressing individual freedom and initiative.

Continuance of Public Education

Why, then, do we taxpayers spend the billions of dollars that we do on public education? There are two main reasons for public education. The first is what Milton Friedman calls the "neighborhood effect," or improving our social environment through education. The second is that of expense and habit. The average family cannot afford the cost of private education and our tax system has become adjusted to financing education.

The "neighborhood effect" is based upon the principle that a family without children should be willing, through its taxes, to support schools for the children of others in order to minimize the social costs of uneducated children, and therefore unemployed adults, who would be a burden on society. Another good analogy is driver education. Young people who have a state-required course in driving are less apt to have accidents which may kill or injure their neighbors. Therefore, it makes sense for the state to require driving instruction of all youngsters.

What then, beyond driving instruction, does the government have the right to require of schools in return for tax money support? While we must maximize free choice, there are certain minimum requirements which governments have a right to demand. These are the three R's. The ability to read and write, add and multiply. We also need a minimum of instruction in citizenship so that our future voter will not only be able to pull the lever on the voting machine but know the effects of his action. That's all!

That's all? There will be many other choices available in our educational system but these will be *choices,* and the state should not be able to require them nor should the state be able to require their presence in the list of options. Immediately we must confront our own intolerance. For the Liberty plan to work, we must achieve unanimity about schools through permission of free choice. You may say, "What about health education, shouldn't it be required?" What about it? The Christian Scientists are going to be opposed. Anti-Sex Educationists are going to violently oppose some aspects of health education. So most schools will have their own version of health education available but no student will be required to take it, nor will all schools be required to offer the subject. Compulsory home economics for girls? Ask a Woman's Libber what she thinks of this!

Federal Role

The basic premise of the Liberty idea is that we should aid those we desire to help—the children—and not the schools. This is a long way from the existing situation on the federal and state level. Although our Constitution reserves the responsibility of conducting education to the states, something took place on October 4, 1957, to change all that factually if not legally. The something was Sputnik, the Russian earth satellite. The orbiting Russian space vehicle was alleged to be twenty times more powerful than our space race entry called Vanguard.

Then a strange thing happened. The American people, instead of blaming their politicians, generals, and bureaucrats for this defeat in the one-upmanship of the cold war, somehow became convinced that their education system was at fault. We apparently hoped we could educate enough scientists and harness some mystical energy they would then possess to thrust ourselves into space in front of the Russians.

Doomsayers and educationists pointed out that one third of all high school students qualified for college had failed to continue because of lack of funds. Surveys were said to show that colleges and universities were having grave difficulties in filling faculty vacancies and the proportion of top quality faculty members was declining. Ultimately and not surprisingly, we passed the National Defense Education Act (NDEA) of 1958. By the time Neil Armstrong set his foot on the moon the investment in education through this act reached nearly $3 billion.

While the pot was still boiling and education's establishment had their foot in the door, our elected representatives passed the Elementary and Secondary Education Act of 1965 (ESEA). ESEA did for elementary and secondary educators what NDEA did for higher education.

In 1974, we passed and the president signed Public Law 93-380 which both extends and expands the earlier NDEA and ESEA. Here are some of the things that our Federal government now does in education:

- Funds are allocated to schools (not students or parents) based on numbers attending whose family incomes fall below the poverty level, and other activities. Cost annually: $1.6 billion, and this new bill may increase that.
- About $600 million for "impact" aid to school districts whose enrollments may have been increased by nearby governmental and military installations. This may have had some validity in time of war, but now it makes little sense. Personnel in nearby government installations live in houses like we do and pay real estate and sales taxes like we do. So the impact is limited to those few cases where military personnel living on base send their children to the local public schools.

- Undetermined millions for projects such as the Metric System; Gifted and Talented Children; Community Schools; Career Education; Consumer Education; Women's Educational Equity; and Elementary and Secondary School Education in the Arts. All of these programs sound great, except that the money should go to parents and students, letting them decide which programs will be of value to them.
- More millions for Adult Education, Education for the Handicapped, Indian Education, and Aid to Schools involved in desegregation.
- Up to $128 million for the National Reading Improvement Program.
- More millions for the odds and ends too numerous to mention here.

There are other ways that our Federal government subsidizes schools. A substantial one is the Department of Agriculture with milk and school lunch programs. Another is the Department of Labor with CETA or Comprehensive Employment and Training Act. Still another is the Department of Defense with ROTC programs, subsidizing both the student and the school. Finally we have the Veteran's Administration with the GI bill, the only program that aids the student and not the school. And "the child is not the mere creature of the state!"

The states did not much object to the Federal Government's poaching on their constitutionally protected preserve, probably because a good deal of the money went through the hands of the state bureaucracy. With the Liberty plan, the Federal Government would be limited to providing the same funds it now dispenses but they would be funneled through the state's voucher program. The tiny remaining bureaucracy could be involved with statistics, a very few research projects, and the provision of information about education for the Congress and the states.

State Role

What do the states do with regard to education? States define goals of education. The high sounding goals of the states are remarkable alike—and as ineffective. As an example, let's look at one for Massachusetts:

Respect for the Community of Man
Education should provide each learner with knowledge and experience which contribute to an understanding of human similarities and differences and which advance mutual respect for humanity and for the dignity of the individual.

They look upon the role of the State as Florida does:

Role of the State in Education
1. To establish state-wide educational objectives.
2. To establish objectives which shall receive highest priority for given time periods.
3. To establish a sound program of financial support.
4. To provide efficient coordination and distribution of funds.
5. To establish minimum standards for achievement and quality control.
6. To assist localities in evaluating results.
7. To develop a good information system on the facts and condition of education.
8. To provide incentives to local school systems and institutions to go beyond minimum performance.
9. To make available to local school systems consultative services which they cannot reasonably provide from their own resources.

The Florida Legislature in 1968 instructed the commissioner of education: "The Commissioner shall expand the capability of the department in planning the state's strategy." No state department of education need be told to expand. That's an unwritten law. In cooperation with the state education association (teacher's union) they search for new programs which can be required of local school systems, providing employment for teachers, administrators, coordinators and evaluators. An example is career education. It has been required by some states for years and was just recently mandated by Michigan.

Definition:

Career Education. Career education shall provide the experiences necessary for each learner to acquire the knowledge, skills, and attitudes to make career development decisions. Such knowledge, skills, and attitudes shall be the maximum the learner's abilities and motivation allow. The career development decisions shall maximize the learner's self-realization, social effectiveness, economic productivity, and moral responsibility. As a result, each learner shall carry out social roles and achieve an active, productive, and satisfying life.

Career education experiences should result in knowledge of one's self and one's environment. They should prepare one to use knowledge and make wise career decisions. They should result in proven competence.

Florida, 1973

Could that be "big brother" talking? Why must a state department of education *order* a local school system to implement a program? Parents and local school districts may have more pressing priorities for which they would like to spend their money.

Establishment education thinks that it knows better than parents what parents want in schools. A powerful lobby, this establishment is able to impose school programs from the state and Federal level, without the advice and consent of parents. When asked, ordinary folk will define career education as vocational education, such as teaching the skills of carpenters, auto mechanics, beauticians, etc., far different from the above. This is not to say that career education is without merit. It is a valuable program, but parents may have other ideas. They resent the condescension with which programs like this are imposed on them by means of a semantic shell game.

A similar example is the currently popular "community education." The announced aim is to use school facilities for community purposes such as pre-schools, adult education, other school activities for students, senior citizen activities, etc. Thoughtful citizens will ask, why haven't schools been doing this all along? To some extent they have had programs with these aims, and it is well that we have renewed emphasis on this utilization of our school investment.

But we must understand that the genesis of the current pressure for community education is not to provide a needed service. Although many public spirited citizens have been enlisted in the promotion of this program, the education establishment looks upon it as a source of employment for coordinators, directors, etc. With the enrollment decline, a "grass roots" movement toward community education can provide funds and employment at state teachers' colleges teaching educators the secrets of community education. State grants or matching funds are then used to encourage school districts to hire coordinators and assistants. How can state legislatures resist the clamor for earmarked appropriations for community education when just about everyone seems to favor it? Meanwhile, funds for schools' basic purposes suffer.

Some State Departments of Education select the textbooks for all schools in the state. This can provide another source of friction. We are all familiar with the bookburning, riots and wildcat strikes in Kanawha County, West Virginia. The Wall Street Journal, in an October 7, 1974, editorial, "The Schoolbook Rebellion," [13] characterizes this eruption:

> The deeper motive of the protestors seems to be resentment—against the schools, the bureaucrats and the upper classes in general. 'Even hillbillies have civil rights', reads one sign. The immediate protest was aroused by what appeared to them as an especially condescending attempt to revise their cultural outlook—by what was, in fact, an unconscious and thus all the more condescending attempt to revise their cultural outlook.

> * * *

> . . . but to these parents they symbolize the judgment of some state bureaucracy that their own pietistic, moralistic way of life isn't adequate. The books were selected to follow state orders that classroom materials 'must accurately . . . depict and illustrate the intercultural character of our pluralistic society.' One Charleston defender of the books stated, 'They help prepare kids to take on life as it is, which isn't exactly like we want it to be.'

> * * *

> So you introduce students to Eldridge Cleaver and the world of convicts and prostitutes. We don't object to these books, but we do feel this viewpoint distorts life even more than the other. Cleaver to the contrary, the average black experience in the 'ghetto' would probably be that of a hardworking, church-going

family trying to raise children right in spite of surrounding vice. Religion would play a major role in their life, and we think the people of Kanawha County would understand them well.

We do not condone book-burning under any circumstances, but neither should we condone the contempt of those in charge for the beliefs of any group in our society. With the Liberty Plan in Kanawha County, the protestors would undoubtedly send their children to a school that suited their moral standards. It is difficult to see that this would in any way endanger the public purpose of education.

The State Department of Education should have no control over the selection of textbooks, the length of the school day, or the number of days in the school year. It would provide a very minimum supervision of the Liberty School Sector, overseeing their functions of voucher distribution and effecting coordination between adjoining Sectors.

Another important task of the state would be to protect against fraud in the operation of schools, and here we have to be alert for politically motivated decisions. Overzealous administrators can tend to eliminate schools which have a philosophy opposed by the board or administration, or where the ownership or management is on the wrong side of the fence politically. Conversely, loose administration can encourage schools featuring useless courses or ownership which has a record of bilking the public in other lines of endeavor. To eliminate self-serving decisions, the ultimate board to which decisions of administrators are appealed should not have more than 50% educators as members.

States now certify schools under the GI bill and the experience and procedures developed will assist in the Liberty Plan. Private trade schools are now required to be bonded. Of interest is the state's experience with the GI bill after World War II. At that time, books and equipment were billed as extras to the state and some schools took this as a "license to steal." Under the present, revised procedure, all funds go to the veteran as they would under the Liberty Plan, and excessive charges have ended.

Certification and tenure would be a function of the schools themselves. Although the state may coordinate the portability of teachers' retirement benefits, increasing the mobility of teachers, they would have no part in funding or administering these plans. Actual operation of retirement plans can be in the hands of voluntary associations or insurance companies.

The State Department of Education would determine the dollars available for vouchers from state, federal and local sources and recommend to the legislature the size of the vouchers for elementary, secondary and higher education, with increased vouchers for special-education students.

One important function, described in the next chapter, would be to provide and administer, through the sectors, achievement tests which will give parents a tool, doubtful though it may be, to tell them what they are getting for their money. These tests should be given in all schools cashing vouchers.

8. Tests and Grades: Take With Grain of Salt

THROUGH THE EYES of parents, let us take a look at tests given to students to determine how well schools, teachers and students are doing (achievement tests) and tests given to students to tell how well they *should* do in school (IQ, SAT or College Boards). Also, we will consider the grading systems used in schools to inform students how well they have learned their subjects, and the controversies surrounding these systems. Tests and grades can have value for parents, if regarded with a healthy skepticism.

Under the Liberty plan, it is important for parents to have some way to select schools other than by recommendations of friends, inspection, reputation, or the puffery of school catalogs. Achievement tests help fill this need.

Achievement tests of one kind or another are now in use in over thirty states, the District of Columbia, Puerto Rico and the Virgin Islands. Although the program is in its infancy, it can be an important force in improving schools, both now and when the Liberty plan is implemented. These tests, when used as a measure of performance for school systems, schools, and classes, are an important means of determining whether you are getting your money's worth. For individual pupils, they are important because the teacher can plan changes in curriculum or teaching methods in order to correct deficiencies evidenced by the tests, of the class or by individuals.

Types of Tests

Objective-referenced achievement tests seem to be the best type because the objectives can be reasonably related to the objectives of parents and/or the state. Michigan's 1973 tests were developed by a committee setting up objectives which they thought should be attained before the fourth and seventh grade levels. At the fourth grade level, in mathematics, two of the 35 objectives are: Telling Time; Indicate a Number that is a multiple of two. In Reading, two of the 23 objectives are: Match words with definitions; Alphabetize words through the first three letters.

These seem to be reasonable objectives for children starting in the fourth grade. If the pupil cannot meet simple objectives like these, then something may be wrong with parents, pupils, teachers or schools. Test results are available for pupils, classes, schools, districts and the state as a whole.

Statewide, 89% of the fourth graders could tell time but only 60% could match words with definitions, with vast differences between districts. The results are useful because they pinpoint subject areas where additional emphasis is needed. Teachers and parents are given an opportunity to correct deficiencies. What school people do not like, however, is the idea of comparing teachers, schools and districts, which is, of course, what the tests should do if they are to be a public service.

There are other factors besides the efficiency of schooling which affect the scores. Social-economic status (SES) appears to have a correlation with the test scores; expectations are a factor; that is, if parents, teachers and fellow students expect Johnny to do well—he does well. Genetics, or how well the children choose their parents, is another factor. However, when the SES is about the same and the percentage point spread shows more than a slight variation in the scores, then one teacher (school, district) is doing a better job than another.

Educators are often embarrassed and secretive about these test results. Michigan tests are constructed and the results expressed so that comparisons between schools and districts are difficult. In other words, they attempt to make the tests not do what they are supposed to do: provide comparative data.

With Michigan's 1973 test results, the average number of students attaining the objectives gives us some rough and reasonably reliable figures on school districts (fourth grade):

	Math	Reading	Instruction Dollars Per Pupil (Elementary)
State of Michigan	76.7	54.9	
Bloomfield Hills (Top District)	90.6	80.1	$686.00
City of Detroit	61.6	36.5	734.00
DeTour (Upper Peninsula)	80.6	52.8	498.00

We can see that affluent Bloomfield Hills comes out on top. This is the SES at work. With wealthy, well-educated parents we can expect this. But if another district with a similar SES has a substantially higher or lower average percentage attaining the objectives, then the difference would be meaningful to parents deciding on schools.

Note that the City of Detroit, although spending more than any other district, has a score 20% less than the state average. The school system blames its low scores on the high percentage of minorities (74%, mostly black) and not enough money. Can this be a cop-out? The most important factors here may again be the SES and the above mentioned "expectations" of the parents, teachers and community. This situation, as indicated by achievement scores and corresponding dollar allocations, cannot be corrected by simply adding more money to the budget.

Detroit spends 47% more than the DeTour school system, in Michigan's Upper Peninsula wilderness, yet DeTour has a low SES and about 12% minorities, mostly American Indians. Could it be that DeTour's staff and population were not listening when they were told "it can't be done"?

If we are going to get our money's worth out of schools, we need more comparisons like this. Admittedly, these scores cannot be considered to have a direct relationship to quality of schooling. Other factors about the school should be considered. But if this is the case, why did Michigan's educators make every effort to keep the results secret?

In previous years, Michigan had used "criterion-referenced" tests which showed only a small difference between schools. In announcing these new "objective-referenced" tests, and relating them to assessment and evaluation, Dr. John W. Porter, State Superintendent of Public Instruction, declared the tests would answer the question "What are we getting for our tax dollar?" Of course, some schools do a better job than others, just like doctors, grocery stores, or gas stations. But the very idea that schools falling below average in scoring are doing a below average job, however true, is unacceptable to most educators.

These new tests were thought to be structured to indicate the attainment of minimum objectives by 85% of the state's pupils. The coverup started when the results came in, and few school districts had attained the desired results.

"DANGER: Assessment is Abroad in the Land" is the title of an article addressed to the state's educators by Frank B. Somer, consultant, Bureau of School Services, the University of Michigan. "[The test results] . . . may in fact, be interpreted to mean that not a single school district in this state is meeting minimal objectives in reading and mathematics." Mr. Somer goes on to urge that no such interpretation be made!

Dr. Thomas Fisher of the State Department of Education, before a group of educators: Test results were "not designed for laymen, PTA's or School Board members." He further cautions that these people "might arrive at interpretations of the data that you don't want them to have."

Test results for districts, schools, classes and individual students were complete for months but were kept secret at all levels. Attempts to get the results were a futile and exasperating experience. If our educators spent as much time and energy improving schools as they spend dodging requests for this kind of information, we would have some fantastic schools. Test results like these should be made public promptly at all levels, except individual, in an understandable form. Parents and the media should insist on this. Individual pupil results should not be made public but given to parents with a brief explanation so they may understand their child's progress and be able to provide help in some areas. There is no reason for secrecy. Citizens are uneasy when information about the performance of public institutions is concealed. When officials say the information is not released because parents cannot understand it, parents naturally resent the inference that they are stupid.

Under the Liberty plan, test results like these would be available from the state to help parents judge their schools. Tests should cover only the basic material in the state-ordered curriculum. But parents must be aware that overemphasis on the tests results can result in teachers "teaching to the test," student trauma, etc.

Another test frequently cloaked in secrecy is the IQ test. IQ tests are supposed to indicate intelligence, but they really indicate things that test specialists think have a *correlation* with intelligence, such as success in school, business, or the military. Some claim that, since the test questions are based on white, middle class experiences, they contain a racial bias against blacks.

If your child is ten and the test result shows him performing at the level of a twelve year old, this gives him an IQ of 120. In the same way, if his score is that of an eight-year-old, he has an IQ of 80. The "average" child is supposed to be at 100. If a child with an IQ of 100 is performing better than average, he is an overachiever and, the other way around, an underachiever. IQ's can increase through normal maturity and by special lessons aimed at teaching how to take IQ tests. The newer IQ tests have more diagnostic capabilities and can be used to plan a curriculum complementing the youngster's abilities.

One objection to the use of IQ tests is that when scores are made available to teachers and parents, who are human, they tend to expect those with low IQ's to do poorly. Since children are unconsciously very discerning, this expectation is satisfied by these students—who then proceed to learn poorly. However, if we can remove the veil of sanctity from the IQ and regard it as an *indicator,* not an ironclad specification of children's abilities, then we will have many more overachievers. Despite the foregoing, parents should demand that IQ scores be made privately available to them, and the figures should be given to the students themselves in upper secondary and college years.

Parents, particularly black parents, had best ignore the current debate sparked by two professors, Jensen and Herrnstein, who claim that the Irish and Negro peoples have lower IQ's than English and American whites. Even if true, we should be concerned with individuals, not races, and it will remain true that some black children are smarter than some white children and vice versa. The color of the individual's skin should not make any difference to him or his school.

Many of us can recall our reluctance to respond to Hitler's "solution to the Jewish problem." Our equivocation at that time not only resulted in attempted genocide but in the cauldron of World War II. Should racists attempt to use Jensen and Herrnstein as a reason to segregate schools, we should respond vigorously and at once.

Another test that supposedly predicts success in school is the SAT or Scholastic Aptitude Test, also known as "College Boards." They seem to be effective in predicting (with many exceptions) how well a student will do in college, particularly in the first year at liberal arts colleges. After the first year, or in technical colleges, the correlation drops sharply. Since they make no allowance for the student's determination to succeed, SAT's encourage some students to go to college who should not go and prevent or discourage others who should go. As with other tests, parents and students should have access to the results, which they should regard with a healthy skepticism.

There is another type of test, called the CLEP for College Level Examination Program. Students can take the examinations and receive credit for classes they have never attended. Some high school graduates earn an entire year's credit before entering college. There is no reason why learning from any source, experience, individual study or alternative-type schools, should not provide the student with credits necessary for the employment credentials he seeks in school. Requirements that make the student sit in a class a specified amount of time in order to qualify for a job, without knowledge gained, are too high a price to pay for "education." Therefore another type of test, one that we should but do not have, would be called SLEP, or School Level Examination Program. Like CLEP for college level, these examinations should provide the student with credit for secondary school courses, where knowledge or skill has been attained from nontraditional sources. Such procedures could be easily integrated into the Liberty School program.

We already have the GED, or General Educational Development Test at the secondary level, which certifies the "equivalency" of a high school education. In some areas, this is one way a student who sometime earlier had dropped out can get an Equivalency certificate that for some employers is comparable to a standard diploma. These types of tests should become standard, rather than exceptions.

Grades

There is nothing sacred about our traditional marking system. Opponents say it is dehumanizing, anxiety producing and authoritarian. In the last ten years there has been a controversial trend toward marking students as either passed or failed as opposed to A, B, C, D, E or 1, 2, 3, 4, 5 or percent grades. The pass/fail approach represented a break with tradition, an opportunity for younger educators to innovate. The pass/fail is criticized because it reduces student motivation to excel. Critics feel that most students will not exert themselves if they have no way of determining the success of their efforts. Where achievement of students is determinable, application is bound to increase.

This controversy has generated a lot of heat and the pendulum seems to be swinging back to a traditional grading system. Were I considering a school for my children today, I would ignore the grading system, believing that there are many more important factors. Children seem to have a sixth sense about their classmates' achievements, so that competition exists despite the pass/fail system.

Tests and grades really produce little heat compared to integration and forced busing, which we will consider in the next chapter.

9. Integration—Forced Busing

SEGREGATED SCHOOLS ARE largely a function of segregated housing. The busing controversy arises from the forced transportation of black students from black areas to white areas, and vice versa, to achieve a numerical integration.

We all have a great deal of compassion for the poor and the disadvantaged. But with sponsors of forced busing, the compassion takes the form of feelings of superiority, of knowing better what is good for the poor than the poor do themselves. They believe in egalitarianism of a sort that would eliminate inequalities of family background, aptitude, ability, determination and luck. But a large majority of us Americans are opposed to social policies that aim for this sort of equality. We think that everyone should be equal before the law and have a reasonable equality of opportunity in education and in access to jobs and housing. But that's about where it ends.

In effect, busing attempts to eliminate forced segregation by forced integration. It is also an attempt to punish children for the sins of their elders, who in the past may have wrongfully arranged school districts or school attendance areas along racial lines. We could break up the neighborhood living patterns that contribute to segregation in housing, but only with laws and state police enforcement that would be contrary to our ideas of a free society.

Force seldom improves understanding or respect, and neither does it improve education. Thoughtful blacks recognize that black students sitting next to white students or suffering the contempt of mobs throwing rocks at their

WALL STREET JOURNAL

Fig. 4. *"Here's one: '4 BR, 2-1/2 bath, close to shopping, guaranteed forced busing to top school in District'."*

*©1973 Reprinted by permission of the *Wall Street Journal* and of the artist, Brenda R. Burbank.

school bus does not provide a quality education. Nor does teaching by white middle class teachers of black ghetto children. Studies made recently by Dr. Jane Mercer of the University of California at Riverside apparently concluded that busing has little or no effect on students' academic achievement.

We can recall the situation in 1959 at Little Rock, Arkansas, when President Eisenhower found it necessary to bring federal troops into action to permit nine black children to attend an all-white school. In this case the school for whites offered a better educational program and re-sources than did the all-black school, a clear case of discrimination against the black children because of their race. But the current busing furor, as in Boston and Detroit, is purely and simply to achieve racial balance, for the black schools and white schools do have equal facilities and the same dollars per pupil.

The judges in the present cases reason that, at some time in the past, school attendance areas and the construction of new schools were deliberately planned to implement segregation. And they are right, of course. Blacks have been damaged by such segregation.

The reasoning then proceeds to correct the damage done to black children of another generation by forced busing of blacks and whites of this generation. In most cases, the segregated attendance areas originally complained of have lost meaning because the schools now get the same amount of money, staff and equipment, black or white. It is difficult, therefore, to see how the furor will accomplish anything for children of any color.

Why the opposition to busing? Public opinion research shows that teaching black and white children in the same school is not the issue. Opposition to busing is not connected to school integration. It comes from a justified fear of violence in ghetto schools. The quality of the school and its environment produce agonizing fears in parents and students alike. With their neighborhood schools, parents feel they at least have a semblance of control. With busing, all control would be out of their hands. And black parents have these same fears.

Parents also fear the quality of education their children will receive in these schools. And they are right. In Chapter 8, Grades and Tests, we show how achievement test results in the City of Detroit are 20% lower than the state average and 30% lower than some of the suburbs! Those in favor of forced busing believe that all black schools, as presently operated, are afflicted with low morale of teachers, inadequate facilities and supervision and low motivation on the part of both pupils and parents. If you will change "black" to "big city," we can say they are right. There was a time when the quality of black schools was due to white racist school officials treating black schools and their pupils as second class. Today, most big city schools are all bad: for blacks, whites and reds and browns. So the problem is to improve the schools for all, and integration by the numbers will not do this. Racial minorities have the same need for diversity in their schooling as the white majority. When all parents have access to the best schools in the state, as a matter of free choice, then the children of black, red and brown parents will have the same educational opportunities as the rich now have.

The Liberty School plan can foster integration and help eliminate racism as a divisive issue in our society. Children who voluntarily go to school together can be expected to live together as adults.

The addition of the scholarship feature to the Liberty plan will encourage the poor to attend schools requiring add-on tuition. Since schools using an add-on will be required to have *at least* 5% scholarship students they will seek out qualified students among the poor minorities to fill this quota.

Critics of the Liberty idea will say that we are tying integration to the school's need for dollars, rather than establishing a mutual desire for true integration. We give tax deductions for contributions to charity—does that debase the motive? There is nothing wrong with using the "carrot" of voucher money to accomplish the high social purpose of integration. It is better than the "stick" of forced busing.

The way we presently distribute tax dollars for schools defrauds the poor of whatever color. Fraud, because it is possible with the same tax dollars to give them a choice of schools that the rich now have: schools that will provide the opportunity to overcome racism, economic and social disadvantage; safe schools; schools children will want to attend; and schools where children will learn.

Give the money to run schools to parents, not to the schools, and you will see schools run effectively, cleanly and without violence. What's more, these children can be given the option of attending many fine schools beyond their neighborhood. These schools will offer a diversity of program to satisfy each student's unique needs.

Inevitably, opponents of the idea of free choice in schools will raise the question: "Are poor blacks, reds and browns competent to choose a school for their children?" The question itself is best described as a racist insult. The poor often are consciously or unconsciously regarded as inferior to the rest of the population, because their skin is usually of a different color; they live in substandard housing; a sizable proportion are on welfare; and they have a higher incidence of crime and more drug users.

But we should look at it this way: How did the poor

get that way? Did they become poor by laziness, by sloven-liness, by lack of ambition? If so, then maybe they should be deprived of the freedom to make choices for their children. But research shows that most of the poor are poor because their *parents* were poor, and because of the disadvantages caused by racial segregation.

Of course the poor are competent to choose a school for their children! They have the strongest possible incentive to make a good choice and use of schools: to break the cycle of poverty.

Will schools patronized by the poor be substandard? Since they will have the same amount of money to spend on schools as the vast majority of parents, they will be able to make good choices. If well-located schools with attractive programs do not exist, competitive forces will soon provide them. What's more, the provision of scholar-ships in expensive Liberty Schools will provide preferential treatment for the poor akin to affirmative action programs in employment.

Some will claim that the poor will choose schools that are fraudulent. That is true. So will members of the middle class and the rich. Despite the supervision of the Liberty School Sector organization, some schools patronized by all races and income groups are going to be incompetent or the outgrowth of radical, untried theories of education. Some schools, public and private, are frauds now, and this may be due to a lack of choice. The poor will not have exclusive exposure to this risk.

Many blacks will choose all-black schools and this should be their right, just as those attending Catholic or Jewish schools have that right. But the schools cannot be all black by discriminatory admission rules, like the Black Muslim schools. Although all-black schools would seem to impede integration, when the blackness stems from free choice rather than compulsion, it can be a source of pride which in the long run will improve the chances for black self-confidence and result in true integration. A case in point is the Dunbar High School in Washington, D.C., which thrived as an all-black institution with high standards from its inception in 1870 to a few years after the Supreme Court's decision in 1954. Then it was "integrated" by edict and today it is like any other violent, big city school. There is no reason to believe that all-black schools might be substandard educationally. Schools that result from the free choice of their patrons are bound to be an improvement over schools imposed on parents by a school board, regardless of the racial makeup.

However, instruction in "Black English" should not be encouraged. If we permit two languages in our society, we will perpetuate segregation. Upward-bound minorities will be competing for jobs with people brought up and educated in the accepted language and culture of our country. Those who would teach Black English do their children a disservice.

The Federal government provides "compensatory" money for schools with disadvantaged children. The idea is to improve the resources of these schools to handle the education of poor and minority children. So far, this program has not proven its effectiveness. In fact, since high-achieving schools do not receive the money, some say that it acts as an incentive for a school not to excel, the exact opposite of its purpose!

P.S. 91 in darkest Brooklyn may have proven the point. The school is too successful for extra money. Reading retardation is only 4% compared with 30% in equally impoverished areas. The principal, Martin Schor, succeeds because he did not believe his peers when they said it could not be done. "My teachers are happy," says Schor, "because they can succeed. They're not eating their hearts out all day."

If we do find that the disadvantaged need and can benefit from compensatory education funds, free lunch, or other assistance, then the financial aid should flow not to the school but to the child whose parents will make a choice of schools. If the poor child comes to school with more dollars attached, then he will be sought after by the best schools.

The Big Cities

Detroit is a good example. The Supreme Court found that the suburban school districts had not been involved in segregating Detroit's schools, so it instructed Detroit Schools to implement a plan of forced busing within the city. Since enrollment within the city is 74% black and other minorities, the 26% white and as many blacks as can afford it are going to flee to the suburbs as rapidly as they can. Parents seeking to regain control over their children's safety and schooling are going to leave the city. A recent survey by the Detroit Free Press shows that 55% of whites and 43% of blacks would leave the city if they could afford it. The result will be a school system with practically all black pupils, in a city that will become an increasingly violence-plagued ghost town. Although a Detroit mayor has no direct authority over the schools, he certainly should seek a solution to reverse the city's deterioration.

Detroit's first black mayor, Coleman Young, will be faced with further decline in his already battered city. Real estate prices will plunge, further reducing tax funds for the city and its schools.

The Liberty plan, with parents free to choose schools, presents a solution for the present emergency situation and provides hope for the future. Students in Detroit's schools would be free to attend any school in the area, public or private, city or suburb. Fear of forced busing would halt and eventually reverse the white flight to the suburbs. With a choice of schools, families would move back to the city to take advantage of the central facilities and proximity to employment. Eventually, Detroit's location as the geographical center of the area might act to encourage new specialty schools, attracting students from all of the suburbs. The city would begin to attract residents, rather than repel them. And at the same time an economic renaissance could begin.

Problems concerning racial integration are among the most serious issues facing our public school system. The simultaneous massive enrollment decline compounds the problem. However, the situation resulting from this birth dearth can be used as an opportunity to help solve some of the problems of the schools. Integration under the Liberty plan would substantially exceed that possible now with the 74% black, and a 26% fugitive white population. Blacks with dollar vouchers attached would be welcomed by suburban schools seeking to maintain enrollment.

10. Where Did the Kids Go?

EDUCATORS AND STATISTICIANS had just about convinced us that we were faced with a school population explosion far exceeding the one that occurred in the 50's and early 60's, when the truth began to rear its persistent head. The preschool population (under five), instead of increasing as forecast, actually declined 15.5% in the decade of the 60's (U.S. Census). Although this decline began to be felt in the schools toward the end of the 60's, school managers either ignored it or ascribed it to a statistical bobble. And the decline continued. In the short time from the April 1970 Census to July 1975 the preschool population declined another 7.3%. All of the indicators,* birth rates and fertility rates, point to an unplumbed depth somewhere below the Zero Population Growth line.

Whether or not this is a long-term trend or simply the deferral of births to a later date, it has serious implications for schools. HEW's Office of Education forecasts a further 9% decline in elementary age population (5-13) and 17% in secondary (14-17) population in the decade between 1973 and 1983.[9] The decline could be much steeper than that in some schools. If the voluntary school-leaving age is reduced to 14 as recommended herein, and by the National Commission on the Reform of Secondary Education; if the present requirements for diplomas and degrees as certifications for employment and promotion are relaxed (Chapter 16), then the effects on secondary schools and

---

*U.S. Bureau of Census *Current Population Reports* Series p-20, No. 277, "Fertility Expectations of American Women: June 1974."

institutions of higher education will be compounded. In the case of higher education, we no longer have a Viet Nam war, propelling students into colleges to avoid draft calls.

Changes in birth rates, except after wars, do not usually swing suddenly and decisively one way or another. Even with an unlikely sudden increase in the birthrate, it would take five years to reach the schools and another six years to affect enrollment, a total of eleven years. For instance, in the Birmingham, Michigan, School District, 787 students enrolled in the first grade, while 1389 graduated from high school. In 10 years, when the present first, second and third graders are in high school, enrollment in high school will drop from the 4048 presently enrolled to approximately 2400.

If the HEW statistics quoted above were uniform in all school districts, schools could cope with the situation. Such is not the case. Many districts have the "empty nester" effect, with parents continuing to occupy the home that earlier housed three or more children long after their children have completed school. Inflating real estate values in suburban districts often make it difficult for young families with children to purchase these homes, which due to school location would be ideal for their children. Therefore, hidden in the averages are some districts, with no land for expansion, which will lose as much as 50% in enrollment. Other school districts, because of new construction, are going to double and triple their enrollment.

One of the effects of this enrollment decline has been to close school buildings and cause unemployment among teachers. And it can only get worse. In good conscience, can we parents ask nonparent and business taxpayers to support a school system which spends most of its money maintaining brick and concrete rather than providing teachers? Can we support the use of critical energy resources to heat or cool half empty buildings? At the same time, the increasing use of the Year Round School may reduce even more the need for buildings and teachers.

It is not easy to close neighborhood schools. Community residents often feel that the local elementary school is a focal point in their lives, and use the school building for many other activities beside education. Without the nearby school, real estate values may decline. Then, too, people fear that the loss of the neighborhood school may result in forced busing to achieve racial integration. "If you must close schools, of course you are not going to close my school, but yours. And if you don't like that, then it must be *his* school," is the most prevalent attitude. For school board members faced with this decision, it is just the beginning of the problem.

Closing neighborhood schools can be a burning political issue. Militant groups are organized to "save" their local school. Picket lines, emotional late night phone calls to board members, recall campaigns, etc. can make life miserable for all concerned. No matter how you juggle the numbers, some school buildings must be closed, unless taxpayers can be convinced to make an even higher contribution per pupil to cover the inefficient operation of half empty schools—a very unlikely proposition.

With present methods of financing schools, if school A is operating at half capacity and school B has a full load, and with both schools on the same program and in the same district, then the parents of school B are subsidizing the parents of school A. The smaller school has fixed costs in administration, maintenance and utilities which on a per pupil basis would nearly double those of the full enrollment school. Yet, if parents want the neighborhood school, they should be able to have it as a matter of choice, but without a subsidy from other parents.

The Liberty plan can defuse this explosive political issue. Some schools will be closed but as a result of lack of enrollment, not by political edict. The Liberty premise of giving the funds to the parents rather than the school, lets parents make the decision as to whether they want a "walk-to" neighborhood school with a minimum curriculum or one further away with an attractive, innovative program.

If parents have a free choice of schools, what choices could be open to them? The possibilities are unlimited. Some may be interested in the year-round school calendars (Chapter 12). Others will be interested in some version of the Traditional, Progressive or Open schools described in the next chapter. Attractive combinations of calendar and program will become available.

11. Shopping for Schools

IF THE LIBERTY plan were in operation today in your state, what school choices could be made available? How would parents choose among the available schools? We first need knowledge of our child, which most of us have to a surprising degree. We need knowledge about the schools which are available or could be available. And we need confidence in our ability to choose. Professional counseling should be available from the Liberty School sector should you wish to use it.

In this chapter we take a quick look at different school concepts, to help you decide which one is compatible with the life style of your family and, more particularly, the learning style of the child. Beyond these concepts you need to consider how close the school is to home (for this is still important); transportation; curriculum; additional tuition, if any; the opinions of patrons; qualifications of the staff; equipment; test results from previous years, etc. Under the Liberty plan, the choice will be yours.

Try to hang a label on a school. It is difficult. As with art or gourmet cooking, it varies with the artist or the chef. But parents are not interested in labels; they want some way to decide which of the schools available to them is best for their children.

Schools can be classified as traditional, progressive or open. The output of a traditional school may be measured as skills in reading and math; a progressive school as the ability to ask questions; the open school as self-knowledge.

Another approach might group schools like this:

Traditional: basics, fundamentals, self-contained

classroom, graded schools, neighborhood school, didactic teaching, structured classroom.

Progressive: team teaching, IPI (individually prescribed instruction), IGE (individually guided education), discovery method, CAI or CBI (computer assisted or based instruction), Nongraded school.

Open School: free school, alternative school, open classroom, school without walls, informal learning, integrated day, Leicestershire plan, open plan school.

Of course, elementary, grade, junior high, middle, high, year round, neighborhood and nonpublic schools may be any of the above.

Of the several reasons for having a choice in schools, the foremost is the differences in children. Pupils from a family living an ordered, disciplined life might not thrive in a school encouraging student control and a high degree of individual initiative with minimum teacher supervision. Conversely, students from a family encouraging an open lifestyle will have trouble with a school having a structured, highly disciplined organization. This is an oversimplification, of course. There are many different shades between.

Of course, not all the individuality of children arises from family structure. Genetic and other factors, some of them unknown, enter into the difference.

Neil Postman and Charles Weingartner in their *School Book*[10]:

> The use of the term 'learning style' is intended to help everyone remember that children vary widely in the ways in which they learn. Some, for example, thrive in a situation that is open-ended, with plenty of room for student initiative, but become moody and anxious in a tightly-run, teacher-directed classroom. Others thrive in a conventional arrangement, but are irresponsible and confused in open

classrooms. Unfortunately, we know very little about the various learning styles of children, and in fact we do not even have a decent vocabulary for talking about the matter. But this much is pretty clear: Very often, what we mean by a 'discipline problem' or an 'emotionally disturbed child' is a child who is being forced to accomodate himself to a situation that is simply unreasonable from his point of view. Naturally, such a child appears to be 'bad' or 'stupid', when, in fact, the only thing holding him back is the absence of a situation that supports his way of learning. In other words, the learning situation is the problem, not the child.

Other important reasons for a choice of schools are the effect competition will have on improving the quality of education; the development of new, more effective learning methods and the involvement of teachers in spirited teamwork, doing their job in the way they think it should be done, in a school having a teaching philosophy they can identify with. Our present schools' plant, staff, and equipment can provide this diversity at no greater cost than our present conformity.

Our school leaders are so conditioned to doing everything in bureaucratic ways that they have difficulty understanding the free choice principle. For instance, Albert Shanker, President of the American Federation of Teachers, pointed with pride to the fact that a "panacea" had failed. The "panacea" whose demise so pleased Shanker was a year-round school in Virginia. He points out that *only* 50% of the parents and 45% of the students were in favor of the schedule. Now 50% is a huge number. If 50% of the patrons of a school district wanted the year-round school, or any other program, shouldn't the managers of the school system find a way to satisfy their desires without imposing their preference on everyone? This is what the Liberty School idea would offer.

There are several essentials that parents must have in order to make their choice effective. The first is safe, dependable transportation, if the school is beyond walking distance. Parents and students must be able to reach the school of their choice with minimum use of personal automobiles, and the transportation arrangement must conserve scarce fuel. The second is adequate information, expressed in lay terms, about the organization, philosophy, personnel and programs of the several schools available to them.

The following is intended to give you a quick look at some of the ways to organize schools you may have been hearing about, eliminating the "non speak" jargon that educators use. Any of these can be year-round schools, neighborhood schools, religious schools, or private schools.

Traditional Schools

Although we hear more about the progressive and open schools, by far the majority of schools can be classified as traditional. Supporters of traditional schools believe that they exist primarily to transmit systematic knowledge, devoting a large share of their time to "the 3R's" (or basics)—reading, writing and arithmetic.

Traditional high schools stress academic courses in English, history, mathematics, science and foreign languages, hoping to develop disciplined minds. Many traditional schools include art, music, home economics, etc., which some regard as frills, but these schools are still highly disciplined. The teacher's job is to present lessons clearly and to encourage the students to work hard for good grades. Memorizing is often used and the operation can be described as teacher-directed.

But some traditional schools appear quite different, having absorbed some progressive and open ways. You might expect to see the serried rows of student desks facing the teacher's desk at the front of the room, but some of these schools are organized with clusters of tables and chairs, carrels for private work, and project areas, very much like an open classroom.

Hilda Jones, a principal of such a school, describes her goal as "Meeting the needs of individual pupils by getting them involved in their own learning within a structured framework."

So do not decide for or against a traditional school without taking a close look. It may be far to the right or left of what you expect.

Progressive Schools

Progressive educators minimize the use of textbooks, formal lectures and memorizing. They want students to take a more active part in their own lessons. Student initiative is encouraged and field trips, films, newspapers and non-text books are used.

Team Teaching, another tool, is the teaching of one or more classes by a team of two or more teachers. One advantage is that it gives teachers the advantage of doing what they are best at by a division of teaching duties. The main disadvantage is that it requires teachers to cooperate to an unusual extent. Other innovative teaching means are:

Individually Prescribed Instruction (IPI). A curriculum is prescribed for each child that will permit him to advance at his own rate. A perceptive and dedicated teacher can guide the child and pick materials to stimulate interest. The student seeks out his own printed and/or electronic materials and works on his own. Since teachers here can become little more than librarians, some of the human element is lost. However, the incompetent teacher can do less damage with IPI than with other methods. Additional record keeping is required but this can be handled by volunteers from the community, the students themselves, or by teacher aides.

Individually Guided Education (IGE). Similar to IPI, the IGE concept uses groups of varying ages. Instruction groups are sometimes large, small or one to one, with the teacher providing tutorial help. The student also works independently, as in IPI.

Discovery method. Don't tell the student, let him find out for himself. If you want him to find out about the causes of the Civil War, don't give him a lecture, movie or one of the fine books on the subject, but give him a library and let him dig it out himself. Like J. J. Rousseau: "Put the problems before him and let him solve them himself."

Critics say that it is ridiculous for students to spend all that time looking up things that are already available in a digested form.

Computer Assisted or Based Instruction (CAI or CBI). Information or skills are stored in a computer or other electronic equipment for discovery by the student. Display can be by typed or oral messages, graphics or visual. Subjects like math, English, foreign languages, science, etc. can be learned more efficiently than with a human teacher.

Objections raised are those of teachers' fears of being replaced by machines; student boredom with a machine, and high capital cost of the equipment.

Nongraded School. Theoreticians feel that grades are an obstacle to learning; they give children a sense of failure; and that competence and satisfaction in learning become not as important as high grades. Without grading, many other things about schools might change. Critics say that children have a highly developed sixth sense as to how the other kids are doing, make a joke out of the nongrading, and argue that there will be less incentive to learn.

Open School

Open classroom? Open enrollment? Open classroom (school, education) is a way of learning, not teaching. Open enrollment is the availability of schools to students without geographical limits.

Here is what Charles Silberman, in his *Crisis in the Classroom*[11] has to say about "opening" the schools: "The 'necessity' that makes schooling so uniform over time and across cultures is simply the 'necessity' that stems from unexamined assumptions and unquestioned behavior. The preoccupation with order and control, the slavish adherence to the timetable and lesson plan, the obsession with routine qua routine, the absence of noise and movement, the joylessness and repression, the universality of the formal lecture or teacher dominated 'discussion' in which the teacher instructs an entire class as a unit . . ."

According to Vito Perrone of the University of North Dakota: "Advocates of open education argue, for example, that learning is a personal matter that varies for different children, proceeds at many different rates, develops best when children are actively engaged in their own learning, takes place in a variety of settings in and out of school and gains intensity in an environment where children—and childhood—are taken seriously."

Annemarie Roeper, headmistress of an open school, Roeper City and Country School, Bloomfield Hills, Mich., says: "Learning is an activity: It is something a child does, not something that is done to him. When a child increases his skills, it is because he does the learning, rather than the teacher does the teaching."

Although open schools are regarded as the newest thing in education, the idea may not be as new as some think. A recent magazine article quoted a teacher as saying, "The children and I are learning together. I don't have any big philosophy of teaching and I don't have the time to prepare individual lessons for each of the (children) in advance. We just take it a day at a time. All I want to do is to help each of them learn as much as possible every moment of the day."

The teacher was far removed from discussion about open education. She had not heard about it. She was teaching in a one-room country school.

To understand an open classroom, visualize a classroom of the size you are used to, but take out the rows of desks facing the teacher. Instead, think of the perimeter of the room informally divided by movable screens, shelves or bookcases into areas which may be (on some days) a reading center, a language arts and listening center, a science center, a math center, a drama area and a woodworking area. In the center of the room are tables with chairs for other activities.

Architecturally, the room may have a door on it and the door may be open—this doesn't make it "open." In fact, the "room" described above may be just one corner of a large area with no walls other than the outside.

Teachers get to know individual children better. Without rigidly drawn lesson plans, students can bring more of their own individuality into the learning process, keeping the teacher intellectually alive and participating. Underneath there still should be a structural thread, with children making a commitment to themselves and to the teacher to learn certain things by a certain time.

Teachers find working in an open classroom stiuation rewarding but physically and psychologically tiring. For

this reason many open-type schools begin with great enthusiasm and then run out of momentum after a few years.
The plan for an open school should be carefully drawn,
with long-run feasibility built in. It must be recognized
that teachers and pupils will need time to adjust by gradually
"opening" the classroom.

The Wall Street Journal[13] thinks that these schools are

A Growing Trend—A few years ago, schools like
this were mostly private utopian ventures with no
money. Most flopped fast. But today, 400 to 600
public high schools operate 'free' or 'alternative'
schools, up from 'maybe 100' two years ago and
from two or three five years ago, says Mario Fantini,
dean of the school of education at the State University of New York in New Paltz. Generally speaking,
officials say such schools don't cost the system any
extra money.

Critics who find 'Progressive' schools mildly
annoying are aghast at free schools, which they
consider hotbeds of self-indulgence. And even en-
thusiasts concede that free schools aren't for every-
body. But many educators think that alternatives
can provide at least one cure for the boredom and
sloth that afflict many high school students.

Schools in Pasadena, California, have organized both
a Fundamental (Traditional) and an Open school, bracketing
the standard, middle-of-the-road program in the other
schools. The curriculum in the Fundamental school is strict
and basic, features the old math, homework, table manners
in the cafeteria, a dress code, quiet, and control. This school
has a voluntary enrollment of 1700 pupils, with a waiting
list of over 1000.

In the Open school, barefoot students dressed in blue
jeans decide for themselves what they want to learn. No

tests, no grades. Teachers gauge the students in terms of their creativity. Enrollment is 550 and the waiting list stands at 515.

If you prefer one or the other of these two school concepts, then you must be willing to tolerate parents who choose the opposite. This tolerance will encourage the diversity we need.

The Liberty idea will permit other school options, such as career education, one of the currently popular crusades of innovative educators. Another is the Year-Round school, which we will look at in the next chapter in its several forms.

12. Year-Round Schools

"GREAT, I LIKE it." "Good because you get more vacations." "Better than September to June." "A lot of fun." These are some of the comments of elementary children after their first year in Northville, Michigan's year-round school.

Enrollment on a voluntary basis started at 171 in August, 1972 and by fall 1974 had reached over 800, 50% of elementary enrollment.

Interest in year round schools (YRS) or extended school year (ESY) originated with districts facing a rapid enrollment increase, without funds to build new schools. With most YRS calendars, the capacity of a building can be increased by one quarter to one third. One study shows that 20% of school districts plan on having a YRS in five years and 38% plan on one sometime in the future. Although the original intent was to save construction costs, the program also is saving operating costs, has substantial academic advantages and is liked by an increasing number of parents, teachers and pupils.

In this chapter, we present year round schools, not as a mandatory, statewide rule, but as a Liberty School option which parents should be able to choose if they find the idea attractive.

One of the most popular types of YRS is the 45/15 program, particularly at the elementary and junior high level. With this calendar students attend school nine weeks and then have a three week vacation, in addition to Christmas, Easter, etc.

The schedule is staggered so that only three of the four

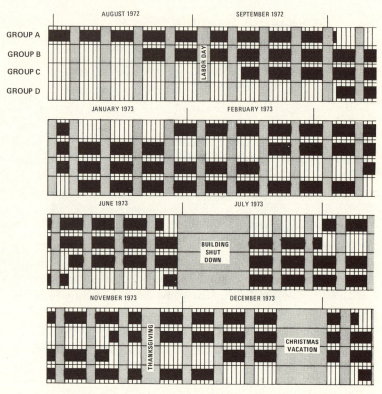

Fig. 5. *45/15 Year Round School Schedule. Only three of four groups A, B, C and D are in school at one time, yet all four groups receive the same number of school days as in the traditional nine month calendar. Thus the school serves one third more pupils, reducing capital investment and, to some extent, operating costs.*

groups or tracks are in school at any one time. Each youngster receives four 15 day (three week) vacations per year. Some schools provide optional "intersession" instruction during the 15 day periods for enrichment or remedial work.

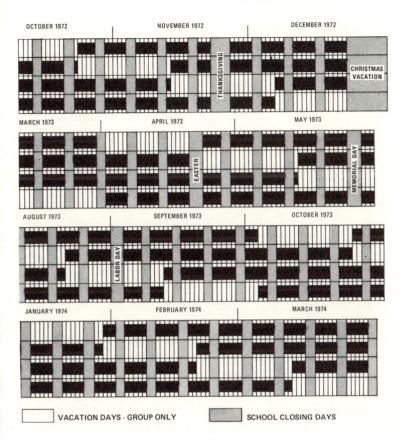

OCTOBER 1972   NOVEMBER 1972   DECEMBER 1972

THANKSGIVING

CHRISTMAS VACATION

MARCH 1973   APRIL 1973   MAY 1973

EASTER

MEMORIAL DAY

AUGUST 1973   SEPTEMBER 1973   OCTOBER 1973

LABOR DAY

JANUARY 1974   FEBRUARY 1974   MARCH 1974

VACATION DAYS - GROUP ONLY   SCHOOL CLOSING DAYS

Parents involved in the 45/15 calendar say the four staggered vacations are more in line with their mobile life styles, permitting economical vacations at off-peak times. They can take family ski vacations, and since one of the four three week vacations occurs in the summer, can still send children to a camp or take them on a traditional summer vacation.

The shorter 45-day instructional periods minimize student fatigue and boredom. Since learning retention is better after only a 15 day vacation, review time can be cut back or eliminated.

The 45/15 calendar is for contemporary people. The old calendar was designed for the land, for farmers who needed their children at home to tend and harvest crops. The nation has been controlled by the traditional school year. Industry, recreational facilities and family living habits can be freed through the year-round school, improving the efficiency of industrial operations and protecting the environment by spreading out the load on recreational facilities.

Savings in operating costs, without considering teachers on a year-round basis, can approximate 5%. Included are factors like the same number of custodians per building; fewer employees, fewer benefit packages; less building maintenance per pupil; one quarter less busses and their accompanying insurance, maintenance and depreciation; four students using equipment and books previously used by three, and many more.

With year-round schools, high initial costs of computer-based and other electronic learning aids, a major obstacle in the past, can be spread out over one third more students.

Energy requirements would be approximately the same per month as on a nine-month program, but summer air conditioning is at off-peak hours. Air conditioning equipment can be simple individual units for each classroom. Many school districts already have a few air-conditioned schools or buildings, while others have been planned for future installation of central air conditioning. These schools can be used as pilot year round schools with low cost.

The most substantial saving can be in teachers' salaries. It would seem reasonable to assume that teachers should not have to be paid one third more to work the twelve months as opposed to nine, but more like 25% more, a compromise benefiting themselves as well as the school.

Teachers' unions will oppose this partly because of the salary provisions but primarily because it will cause a drop in their membership, increasing the numbers of their members already unemployed due to enrollment decline. They also will object to its effect on teachers' plans to pursue graduate programs which require that they spend a summer in residence on a college campus. But schools in turn can eliminate the contract provisions calling for higher pay for advanced degrees which have shown no correlation with increased competence.

However, as a practical matter, most schools implementing the YRS have found it necessary to have teachers track with students, so that they work only the traditional 180 days per year. Where they do work longer, they are usually paid proportionally more. In the future, with a free choice of schools, some schools will be able to attract more patronage if they are able to cut costs and improve the program by taking full advantage of the YRS cost-saving potential. Thus, the full potential of year-round schools may not be realized at their inception.

In scheduling 45/15 or other year round schools, it may be important to parents that their children at various grade levels be on the same track so that the family may vacation together. This may cause scheduling difficulties.

Some districts organize the tracks geographically. This method can reduce transportation costs because no busses need operate in one quarter of the area at a time. However, it may be objectionable to some parents because their choice of the track or schedule is restricted.

Juvenile vandalism at school buildings has decreased in communities after a year-round school has been initiated, since up to three quarters of the student body is in school during July and August when young miscreants are normally on the loose. Student athletic and extra curricular activities will not be affected if changes are made in qualifying rules; schedule modifications are made, and parents cooperate. Vacation-type job opportunities for students are restricted in a 45/15 program. For this reason, one of the other programs may be the best choice for high schools.

The Quinmester

This calendar has been developed by the Dade County (Miami Area) Florida Schools. The calendar divides the school year into five 45-day or nine-week sessions. A pupil must attend four quinmesters in the five. He has the option of attending all five quinmesters with an early graduation, or of taking any quinmester as a vacation period.

One of the advantages to this is that the community can still use the quinmester school as a traditional 180 day school by going to school only four quinmesters. It is felt that the number of families choosing a vacation other than the summer will increase as time goes on. No plans are being made to make attendance mandatory in certain quinmesters. Used in secondary schools initially, the plan is being extended to elementary grades.

Four Quarter or Quadrimester

Atlanta, Georgia, implemented this program in 1968. The year is cut into four quarters and the program is nongraded; individualized.

Students can choose any quarter for vacation, or none. They can seek early graduation, although few do. Few students take vacation quarters other than the summer. Close to 6000 pupils out of the 32,000 involved work part time. Some student comments: "Going to school all four quarters, I don't get behind and yet I can hold down a part time job." "By taking three or four courses a quarter, I don't feel pushed. We schedule what we feel I can handle without my getting upset and nervous." "I'm on the Annual staff, so I went the fourth quarter to lighten my load all year and give me more time for the yearbook."

Concept Six

This program, started in Jefferson County Schools near Denver, divides the school year into six 45-day periods. Families have the option of taking either vacation pattern A, B or C.

Surveys of student interest indicate that about 50% want to return to school during a vacation period to participate

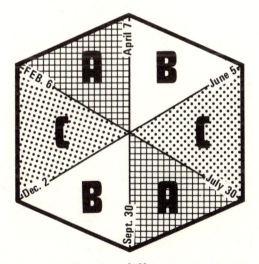

Fig. 6. Concept Six: Six different entry times, as shown above, have the effect of making the curriculum continuously accessible to students throughout the year at the same time reducing the delay of entry for kindergarteners who reach age five after Labor Day. These multiple entry times also make it easier for students who must transfer in or out of school to districts with traditional calendars. Students and their parents will select either vacation pattern A, B or C.

in extra learning. A community survey conducted after a three months' public information campaign indicates that about 80% of parents and staff were in favor of the program. One of the consideration factors used in designing the schedule was to insure that the calendar would still be desirable once the classroom shortages were over.

Many other year round-school approaches are in operation or on the drawing boards. No one of them is best for your schools. A program can be designed for your way of life, climate, and local industries. Unless an overriding classroom shortage requires otherwise, the year-round school or schools should be voluntary.

13. A Temporary Solution: Alternative Public Schools

THERE ARE WAYS that some of the advantages of the Liberty idea can be utilized in our present school system, without waiting for public acceptance of the idea and ensuing legislation.

Despite the increasing interest in ways to provide alternative choices within the public education system, a plan as far-reaching and as necessarily controversial as the Liberty School plan may require several years before it can be fully implemented. Meanwhile, some states and some school districts will wish to go as far as they can toward encouraging free choice in existing public schools.

One estimate has over 3000 elementary and secondary schools that can currently be classified as "alternatives." A projection indicates that we will soon have 20,000 such schools, These options include some types we have not mentioned earlier, like Magnet Schools with a curriculum planned to attract students from conventional schools, sometimes to achieve integration. Schools Without Walls, like the Parkway Program in Philadelphia, use community facilities such as office buildings, Museums, and Public Libraries for classrooms. Drop Out or Drop In Schools are for dropouts or potential dropouts from regular high schools. Disruptive Students Schools not only get trouble-makers out of the conventional classroom but help the students improve their self-image. Outward-Bound schools take students into challenging natural environments, where they learn to get along together and brave the elements. Although these alternative schools do provide different learning-teaching situations for teachers and students, the essential ingredient of the Liberty Plan, competition, is often missing.

There are many obstacles to a temporary approach. Legal problems will prevent the inclusion of private and religious schools. Teachers and administrators are reluctant to become involved in a competitive situation because they regard it as unethical and see in it a threat to future job security. Add-on tuition would not be legal except in the form of voluntary contributions. Strong community pressure with a determined school board and an outstanding superintendent of schools will be required to make such a plan work. But some progress is better than none.

For alternative public schools to work, school systems must encourage a diversity of methods among their schools, realizing that there is no single way to operate schools, but many ways for many different students. Geographical barriers which compel attendance at certain schools must be eliminated. Most important, we must all realize that a school that is not attracting and keeping students has no right to survive.

The basis for a temporary solution would be open enrollment, or the permission for students to enroll in any school beyond their attendance area. This open enrollment, at the minimum, would be in the student's home district. Far better would be open enrollment on a reciprocal basis with adjoining districts or throughout the state. The receiving school would receive the per pupil expenditure from the school sending the students. Of course, this could cause fear and trepidation on the part of school administrators. They will fear the loss of a substantial part of their budget to nearby schools or districts. But the attractiveness of educational programs will improve.

The Liberty School plan of increased autonomy for local

schools will give each principal a budget consisting of the total dollars spent per pupil, systemwide, at the school's grade level. This would include the amount spent for teacher, principal and custodian salaries; for building maintenance; and for other expenses such as heat, light and textbooks.

An approach like this will avoid the subsidy that schools with a large enrollment give, in effect, to schools with a small enrollment. This comes about through the tendency to standardize maximum class size throughout the district. Administrative costs in the district can be reduced with autonomy at the building level. The function of the district's administration becomes less a matter of supervision and more one of providing services which the schools are unable to provide for themselves.

Salaries and expenditures can still be paid by the district and charged against the individual school. However, the allocation of the school's budget between salaries and other expenses should be up to the principal and his community of teachers and parents.

The autonomy of the principal and his community should extend to the program to be offered. By offering attractive and distinctive programs, the school may be able to attract patronage from parents with children attending other schools, even from other districts.

Some of the specific ideas presented in this chapter were developed to fit the conditions in two adjoining suburban Detroit school districts, Birmingham and Bloomfield Hills. Much of this material was published in the local suburban newspaper.

Together, the two districts had 23,573 pupils in the fall of 1973. Enrollment had declined rapidly from a peak in 1967 of 27,458. Further massive declines were expected. The expenditure per pupil, social-economic status, tax rate, and dependence on school buses for the two areas were similar.

Birmingham had closed one school after much rancorous debate and a committee had recommended the closing of three more, but the Board had postponed action hoping another solution could be found. Bloomfield Hills had closed one school with little difficulty because a new school had been built nearby.

Some thought had been given to merging the two school districts due to their geographical dovetailing and similar financial characteristics. However, it did not appear to be politically feasible. The plan was developed based on each district offering open enrollment to the students of the other. To make this open enrollment a practical reality, a system of shuttle buses was worked out so that any student could attend any school in either district. A sketch showing this transportation plan is shown on Page 34.

The principals were to be encouraged to offer a variety of programs including traditional, progressive, open, and year-round. This was to be in response to demand, so that choices would increase as parents became aware of the potential options. To this end, a series of meetings were to be held to explain the different programs and to determine parental and student interest.

Parents who desired a neighborhood school could have this option, and the neighborhood school could become one of the innovators, if the community wished. The idea was to close only those schools which were unable to attract an enrollment large enough for a minimum program. Areawide, the spending of an increasing percentage of the school budget on maintaining buildings would be avoided by giving each school a budget per pupil based on its fair share at the grade level.

For example, let us use an elementary school with a

capacity of 500 and an enrollment of 175. Expectation is that enrollment will further decline next year to 150. Under present plans, the school would be a prime candidate to be closed with the students redistricted to another school. Call this school Small Elementary.

Another school, Large Elementary, might have an enrollment of 500 with a capacity of 600. Budget per pupil in both schools would be $1000.00.

Here's how the numbers might look:

TABLE 1

	Large	Small
Enrollment	500	150
Budget	$500,000	$150,000
Maintenance, Custodians, Supplies Heat, Light, Office Supplies	52,200	37,150
Principal* and Clerical Salaries	33,000	29,000
Substitutes, Instructional Supplies, Supplemental Pay	23,500	8,500
Subtotal	$108,700	$ 74,650
Per Pupil	$ 217	$ 498
Balance of Budget to Teachers	$391,300	$ 75,350
Teachers Available at $15,500**	25.25	4.86
Teachers for Art, Music, Etc.	5	1
Classroom Teachers	20.25	3.86
(With Principal Teaching)		(4.25)
Class Size	25	35

*Since the individual schools have autonomy, each must have a principal. The principal in Small may teach part-time.

**Teachers are billed to individual schools on the basis of the average cost per teacher, systemwide, preventing any one school from being burdened with a concentration of high-salaried teachers. This figure includes fringe benefits and seems high because this district's declining enrollment has caused a disproportionate number of high seniority teachers.

We can see that Small Elementary has a class size of 35 with substandard provisions for art, music and physical education. The principal, with his limited budget, must not only pay teachers' salaries but maintain the building and purchase textbooks and supplies. Both schools can do purchasing through their district office.

If the school board subsidized Small Elementary by adding teachers to keep the class size down, it would do so at the expense of parents in Large Elementary. Since the parents in Small have made the free choice of that school, then they should be willing to accept the large class size. It is either that or send their children to Large or some other elementary school in the district.

The principal of Small does have several alternatives. In addition to using volunteer parents as teacher aides, he can plan a program to attract students from throughout the two-district area, thus becoming entitled to a larger budget. Or, he can ask parents to voluntarily contribute $115.00 per child to a fund which will be used to supplement the district-provided $1000.00 per pupil. Assuming 90% of the parents contribute, one teacher can be employed for a cost of $15,500.00 and class size can be reduced to 27.

Even though pupils may be attracted from other schools in the two district area, there still would not be enough to go around. When enrollment reached the point where schools were spending over one half of their budget (including voluntary contributions) on maintenance and fixed expenses, then the school could be closed. Whatever criterion is used, schools would be closed because of lack of patronage, not by administrative fiat.

Because elementary and secondary schools would have autonomy, diversity would flourish. Programs need not be standardized within the school but several mini-schools can be available.

With two high schools in Birmingham and two in

Bloomfield Hills, plus an area vocational school, it would seem that diversity in choices at the secondary level could be multiplied. This can only be made feasible by a joint transportation operation.

One or more of the schools should be on a Year-Round program, although the 45/15 plan discussed earlier may not be the most desirable for high schools. Along with the 45/15, we should consider the Four Quarter, Quinmester, and Concept 6 with 4, 5, and 6 school periods annually. The program selected should present options for part-time employment, early graduation, choice of vacation period, or no vacation at all.

Each of the four high schools now has some different programs, including graphics, power transmission, office practice and distributive education (retail sales). Community service programs such as nurse's aide, teacher aides, and helpers for the Red Cross, Cancer Society and nursing homes round out the diverse programs available. Many more can be added in each school. With only 10 different programs in each school, the total available becomes 40. Parents, school principals, staff, and students should decide what new courses are added, not the central administration.

The free choice available to parents and students in the temporary plan should be available to teachers as well. This would permit them to choose a school having a teaching philosophy compatible with their own. Since personnel account for 85% of school costs, the next chapter will be devoted to an appraisal of the present situation of teachers and other school people, and how the Liberty plan would benefit them.

14. School People

IT IS NOT surprising that school problems are most often people problems, when we realize that 85% of the budget goes for salaries, with teachers alone receiving 65%. It is therefore easy to start an argument when discussing subjects such as accountability, teacher militancy and strikes, tenure, certification, merit pay and class size. The very nature of the way we finance and control schools assures the insolubility of these difficulties.

The Liberty plan, by giving freedom to both teachers and parents, offers a solution. Teachers will be free to choose schools that have philosophies of education similar to their own; free to be financially rewarded for superior teaching; free to be promoted based on accomplishment rather than academic degrees; free of restrictions causing massive unemployment in their profession; and finally, free to strike. Parents or students will be free to choose a school fitting their learning style and educational objectives, and free of restrictions on how much money they can spend on schooling.

The competence of teaching personnel, at least when first employed, is probably as good or better than personnel in other lines of endeavor. However, the debilitating effects of antiquated promotion policies, tenure, association with mentally retired teachers and, most importantly, the example of older teachers, administrators and unions, means that after a few years, even the best "bright eyed and bushy tailed" young teachers either drift into other lines of endeavor or become dull, gray automatons waiting for retirement.

Teaching is an art, not a science. The enthusiasm of the teacher for his subject and his ability to infect pupils with the vital spark of interest and inquiry is the most important learning ingredient. Class size, textbooks, and buildings are of less importance. Yet this is found in only the most outstanding teachers operating in the most encouraging climate. The vital spark is lost in the shuffle through our present system of continuing to give school money to schools rather than those we intend to benefit—parents and students.

Let's take a look at the problems schools face with school people and how the Liberty Plan will help solve them:

Accountability

The development of any effective system that holds teachers and administrators accountable for their performance within the public schools is unlikely.

Teachers' unions claim that they are in favor of meaningful accountability. In practice they oppose every effort to sort out the good teachers from the bad. They admit that some teachers are not very good and a few are very bad but resist every effort to do anything about it.

Administrators proclaim their dedication to establishing systems of accountability but in reality they, too, are opposed to the principle. They are basically a kindly group who identify with their teachers and cannot bring themselves to give black marks to anybody. While teachers' unions work to make the regulations surrounding accountability ineffective, administrators surround the systems with bureaucratic red tape to insure failure.

If we look at the performance of individuals in civil service, we find few examples of any workable system to weed out the unfit. What makes us think that we can accomplish this objective with schools as they are presently organized?

Under the Liberty Plan politics would be removed from this controversy. Schools and school systems would establish whatever quality controls or accountability provisions for the performance of their personnel that they might deem effective. Management would be limited by its collective bargaining agreements with teachers or other unions, if any. But more importantly, the school would not be able to compete with other schools if its personnel did not perform satisfactorily. A school that could not lead and inspire its teachers would soon go out of business. In the end, the best accountability control is the parent with school money voucher in hand!

Certification

Certification of teachers by state agencies excludes from the profession persons whose experience and competence are most needed by schools. Who can better teach in ghetto schools than one who comes from that background? Yet we consistently bar individuals that are badly needed in schools by outmoded technical requirements. The Supreme Court recently decided a case which gives hope in this area. (see Chapter 16.)

Many people, because of their personality, emotional makeup or other qualities, just will not make good teachers. Present certification requirements make no effort to integrate these things into the decision of whether or not this person can teach. Instead the state agency assumes, in most cases, that graduation from a state teacher's college or accumulation of credits in education makes a teacher.

Postman and Weingartner in their *The School Book*,[10] make the point quite well.

> The situation is comparable to what the Pittsburgh
> Pirates would get if their requirements for making

the team were that an applicant pass a paper-and-pencil test on hitting, running and throwing, and submit a transcript showing that he has successfully passed such courses as Great World Series Pitchers and The History of the National League. Undoubtedly some applicants could do this *and* also hit .310. But you would get a higher number of .185 hitters. And you would never really find out how to prepare men to survive in the big leagues. Happily for Pittsburgh fans, the Pirates do not certify competence in this way. The teaching profession is not yet so enlightened.

With Liberty independent schools, the state would have no right to intervene in the selection of their personnel. The needs of certification, if any, would be handled by the school systems themselves or by private mutual associations.

Critics will allege that children should only be taught by state certified personnel, like doctors and engineers. But one look at the failures of state government in teacher certification will refute that argument.

Tenure

This policy came into being to protect teachers from arbitrary, unreasonable, politically motivated dismissal. Teachers still need that protection and most have it through their unions and by the federal and state civil rights laws. Bascially, what we are talking about is seniority rights, the same thing that industrial workers have in their union contracts. But states do not need to get into the act.

The present situation by Myron Brenton, in *What's Happened to Teacher*[16]:

> If merit pay is a dirty word to most teachers, tenure is almost a sacred one. As it has worked out, tenure is the closest thing to an ironclad promise of job

security with no strings attached. It goes a long way toward making teaching the most secure occupation of any, where professional aspirations are involved. What tenure provides is a guarantee that teachers can't be dismissed from their jobs, except for certain specified causes—usually immorality, dishonesty, willful neglect of duty, or malfeasance. Dismissal is preceded by elaborate due process procedures. These include a hearing, right of counsel, chance to subpoena witnesses, opportunity to appeal, etc.

Although tenure has protected teachers from undue threats and trespass against their civil rights, it has acted to keep salaries low, to encourage mediocrity and to dampen motivation to excel.

Given the political facts of life regarding tenure it is extremely unlikely that the situation can be improved as long as schools are operated by political bodies. If parents have a free choice of Liberty schools, however, teachers and administrators will have a community of interest in creating fair and reasonable seniority agreements.

Merit Pay

As with accountability, it does not stand a chance in our present school environment. Proposals are emasculated by administrators and teacher unions alike.

The merit pay situation is again best described by Myron Brenton:

To qualify for higher pay, teachers must keep on taking additional college courses. With good reason, teachers call them 'cash register courses'. There's no systematic program of professional growth. Sometimes teachers seek out or find courses that help them become more effective instructors; often they don't. Often, tired from the day's grind they take the easiest courses or the ones that fit most easily into their schedules. This is the easy way of setting up criteria for teacher's salary increases, but it does little or nothing to improve their competence."

The popular impression that teachers are overpaid is not true—for the good teachers. They are seriously underpaid and for this reason many do not stay long. The poor teachers are overpaid at any price.

Badly needed are schools which will reward teachers for outstanding jobs, and which have a teaching philosophy they can identify with. Schools should be allowed to seek out better teachers and offer them more money, fringe benefits, freedom to teach, or all three! There is no possibility of doing this within the present public school organization. Only through a system providing a free choice for parents, pupils *and* teachers, can progress be made in schools.

Surplus

Unemployed teachers in the fall of 1974 are estimated at 600,000! Included are unabsorbed recent graduates, teachers desiring to return to the schools after raising a family, and those laid off because of declining enrollment or lack of funds. The school industry is unique with an unemployment rate of over 25%, and it is getting worse!

The number of these actually available for employment is unknown. But the problem can only become worse as falling enrollment works its way through the grades. It is hard to understand an industry which in effect limits the input of funds to hire teachers to only government money, while many are willing and eager to supplement the state funds.

Under the Liberty system permitting a free choice of schools and optional parent-paid add-on tuition, many thousands of additional teachers might be employed. Much of the additional money paid by parents could go to hire more teachers and therefore reduce class size.

Teacher Militancy

The objectives of teacher unions are not the same as their membership. Union leaders strive to increase their powers and perpetuate themselves in office. They aim to expand their powers by demanding, and getting, control over what have been Board of Education prerogatives. They want to control the selection of textbooks, promotion, assignment, transfer, substitutes, school hours, superintendents, after-school activities, building construction, and class size.

We parents will wake up some morning and find that control of our schools has been seized from our elected representatives by the teacher union dictators who are accountable not to the teachers or to the public but only to themselves. Parents are on a collision course with the teachers unions, not the teachers.

Teacher unions elect school board members responsive to their needs through the secret and illegal use of their nonprofit mailing privileges. Candidates for the school board in our area are "screened" by the Education Association and those that pass muster are endorsed and given election help from advertising to distribution of circulars.

It is difficult to see how a school board member can remain loyal to the public purpose when he actively seeks endorsement of a union with whom he is supposed to negotiate at "arm's length" a contract covering most of the school cost.

The National Education Association (NEA) and the

American Federation of Teachers (AFT) and other educator groups have learned how to make friends with state and national political candidates. Their spending on the 1974 election probably exceeded five million dollars. They push to increase Federal aid to education, but this reads increased power for union officials. Rhode Island's Democratic Senator Claiborne Pell, the chairman of the Senate subcommittee on education, said of his 1972 victory, "My election is a victory for teacher power." Guess who pushes hardest for Federal school aid?

The true test of a union by its membership is "What have they done for me on pay day?" Not much, really. If you are a beginning teacher, or only a few years into your career, you have actually *lost* money. Since as a beginner you have little clout in union politics, the bargaining team "sells you out" in favor of higher salaries for high seniority and master's degree teachers.

The starting salary for bachelor's degree teachers in my home district was $8225.00 in 1971. By fall of 1974 it became $9000.00, an increase of 9.4%. Master's degree teachers at the same time went from $16,000.00 to $18,305.00, an increase of 13.7%. But what is important to note here is the *differential* between bachelor's and master's degree salaries of 103%. Does the master's degree teacher have twice the competence of the bachelor degree teacher? Because he has a master's? Because he is older and more experienced? The teaching profession needs answers to these questions; answers that are not likely to be provided by unions dealing with political school boards.

An article by Allen W. Smith in the December, 1972 *Phi Delta Kappan* indicates that teacher negotiations have had little overall effect on teachers' salaries. The ratio of the average salary of public school instructional staff to per capita income in 1961–62 was 2.52, before extensive teacher union bargaining began. In 1970-71, the ratio had actually *dropped* to 2.44!

Could it be that supply and demand has more effect on teacher salaries than unions? Of course there is no doubt that during this period there have been substantial changes in working conditions, such as nonteaching duties, assignment and reassignment, pensions, health insurance, etc. These have all increased school costs substantially but they have not "put meat on the table" for the members as other unions are able to do.

Strikes

Strikes by teachers are prohibited by law in many states. But teachers strike anyway. After the school board dismisses them for striking, they are rehired as part of the settlement.

Education is the only industry where strikes cost the strikers nothing in terms of lost pay. The school year is simply extended and holidays reduced in order to operate the required 180 days. Under this painless procedure, it is a wonder schools do not have strikes more often. And they probably will when the unions realize this unique advantage. It is pupils and parents who pay the price in disrupted family vacation plans, in sweltering July classrooms and in feelings of helpless rage. Yet teachers should have the right to strike, like other employees. However, they should pay the cost in lost pay as other strikers do.

Without the state-mandated 180 or 185 days, strike-caused school closings can mean lost pay to teachers and the value of the voucher could be reduced relative to the number of days on strike.

With Liberty schools and parents free to choose, teacher strikes will be infrequent. The teachers' organization and school management will have a community of interest in pleasing parents. If schooling is interrupted excessively by strikes, parents will simply transfer their children to another school having more stable employee relations.

Administrators

As a group, school administrators are an outstanding element of our public schools. Compared with similar officials in government and private industry, they are hardworking and dedicated to their jobs despite frequent unreasoning criticism. However, the size of the administrative staff seems to grow and grow. Each new program, evaluation, career education, community education, requires a new director or a new coordinator. Seldom is any thought given to someone wearing two hats, or three if need be. Administrators are required to have an education background in positions that instead require leadership, executive, business administration, financial or other abilities.

We parents must understand that the public school environment in which administrators have survived throughout their careers is substantially different than what we propose in this book. So, a lot of firmness, patience and understanding is needed when reasons are given for why schools cannot be changed.

Put yourself in the position of a principal who for years has run his school with every lockstep dictated by higher authority. With little experience or opportunity to exercise his independent judgment, he might suddenly be forced to do things on his own in an autonomous school. A lonely prospect, this future shock.

Remember, too, that we parents have in the past criticized superintendents and administrators if one school had a different program than ours, because we thought we were being discriminated against. Like other public officials, they have learned that there is safety in *not going anywhere alone.* Yet this is what we need. There are administrators with the necessary fortitude to provide this diversity; they need only your encouragement.

15. Higher Education

IN EARLIER CHAPTERS we have avoided discussion of personnel in higher education, because the problems and solutions are unique.

The problems in colleges and universities are two: the lack of equity in the way tax monies involved are distributed, and the lack of efficiency in the operation of these institutions. These problems are soon to be multiplied when the enrollment decline discussed earlier reaches the higher education level. But if the Liberty plan can solve the equity problem, the others will solve themselves.

At the outset we should take a look at the costs of a college education. Parents of public college students not only must scrimp and save to provide their youngsters with tuition, fees, board and room, totalling over $2500.00 per year, but they must pay state and federal income taxes on these amounts as well. The taxes that they have paid go to make up tax-funded cost for publicly controlled institutions.

An additional and often overlooked cost of a college education is the loss of income to the student himself. We can assume that even in the lowest jobs, students could earn at least $5000.00 per year, totaling $20,000.00 for a four-year degree.

A recap of the costs of a four year college degree, in 73-74 dollars, would look like this:

State, Federal and Local Tax Money	$20,000.00
Parent's or Student's Contributions	10,000.00
Loss of Income to the Student	20,000.00
	$50,000.00

After you add the recent inflation, these 73-74 dollars become a cost that the average student and his family can ill afford.

The way we distribute our tax money for elementary and secondary schools defrauds the poor. But the way we apportion the funds for higher education defrauds an even larger group—the vast middle class—while favoring the poor and the rich. If you are poor, and can prove it, there are numerous and ample programs to finance your higher education. If you are rich, and can spare the years, we taxpayers will contribute over forty thousand dollars to let you stay in a college or university for bachelor's, master's and Ph.D. degrees. But, if you are part of the vast tax-paying middle class, you pay the taxes to educate the rich and the poor in a manner you can't afford for your own sons and daughters. Ask for scholarship help and you are told you make too much money!

In addition, should you and your children be able to scrape together enough money to pay the tuition, room and board, etc., the only way your state's higher education establishment will accommodate you is if you attend one of the public institutions in your state! And that's another part of the fraud. The institutions you are compelled to attend are inefficient and cost as much as three times as what you can buy for the same amount elsewhere!*

The inequity in the way we finance higher education is well described by the University of Chicago economist, Milton Friedman:[2]

> The equity argument . . . is particularly clear at
> college and university levels because of the existence
> of a large number and variety of private schools.

*See the discussion of schools of Architecture later in this chapter.

The state of Ohio, for example, says to its citizens: 'If you have a youngster who wants to go to college, we shall automatically grant him or her a sizable four-year scholarship, provided that he or she can satisfy rather minimal education requirements, and provided further that he or she is smart enough to choose to go to the University of Ohio. If your youngster wants to go, or you want him or her to go, to Oberlin College, or Western Reserve University, let alone to Yale, Harvard, Northwestern, Beloit, or the University of Chicago, not a penny for him.' How can such a program be justified? Would it not be far more equitable, and promote a higher standard of scholarship, to devote such money as the state of Ohio wished to spend on higher education to scholarships tenable at any college or university and to require the University of Ohio to compete on equal terms with other colleges and universities?

The unfair way we now finance higher education will doom the smaller private universities. It is doubtful whether private philanthropy can or will continue to support these institutions. Only the rich students can afford the tuition required despite the college's most stringent economies in administration. Most students are drawn to the low-priced (to them, not the taxpayers) public institutions.

The so-called private colleges and universities are no longer private. Independent of public support, yes, but not private for they efficiently educate the public. These schools are open to the public, with only a very few exceptions. A better name for them would be "independent."

Recently, some states have begun to realize the tremendous loss they would suffer were their independent schools forced to close. These states provide lump sum payments for degrees awarded, scholarships for private schools, tax-exempt bond issues for construction, and other grants-in-aid.

But even in these states, the students at most independent colleges or universities are treated like second class citizens. The prestigious independent schools like Harvard, Yale and Princeton and the big state universities get disproportionately large shares of government and philanthropic funds. The result is the poor institutions are getting poorer and the rich are getting richer.

An analysis of HEW's statistics, nationwide, indicates that about $4100 was spent per full time equivalent student per year in publicly controlled institutions of higher education. This includes around $500 from the student for tuition and federal, state, and local tax money. This is an average of poor states, rich states and states-in between for the 73–74 school year.

The inequity is that if you have the $500 price of admission the government will give you $3600 of educational services. *Provided,* you will attend a public institution in *your* state.

You are not given the opportunity to take the $4100 to an institution of your choice. Should you decide to attend a non-public college in your state or a public or non-public college out of your state, then you must not only do so with your own funds but continue to pay the taxes to support others who do attend your state schools—a case of double taxation.

Look at it another way: The student who can afford to stay in the University for eight or more years of undergraduate and post graduate schooling will get more than $40,000.00 in tax money!

If these public institutions that have a monopoly on our tax money were doing a good job, then their possession of a monopoly might be excused on the ground that the monopoly is responsible for the efficiency. Such is not the case.

You may have seen a news item about the sociology professor who held down three full time jobs at two colleges and one university. Do you think that this is quite a feat and possible only if the teaching posts are within a metropolitan area? Actually, one college was 65 miles south of Pittsburgh, another in the Bronx and one university 70 miles north of the Bronx. The efficiency is there, all right, but it belongs to the professor, not to the three institutions.

Let us listen to Professor X in an interesting book, *This Beats Working for a Living, the Dark Secrets of a College Professor*.[17] The author evidently thought anonymity was the better part of valor in saying things like this:

> The professor, in truth, finds only some fifteen to twenty hours of his week filled with actual work related to his duties. Some of them, especially if they live in a city large enough to grant them some anonymity, take a part- or even full-time job off campus; and this is not moonlighting—it is daylighting.
>
> * * *
>
> There are a few professors—human nature being what it is, probably about fifteen to twenty percent—who try to research and write, who really try to work with their students and to keep abreast of their fields, and thus who work forty, fifty, and even sixty hours a week. I have observed that the man truly successful in his field, who gains a reputation for excellent teaching and for wide publication, generally works twelve to fifteen hours a day and much of his weekends. Perhaps this explains the high divorce rate among the really successful academicians.
>
> The college teacher thus can be among the world's laziest people, drawing his salary under false

pretenses while complaining about being over-worked and underpaid or he can be among the world's hardest working individuals. Efficiency experts would not be welcomed on most campuses, however, for the majority of professors would be too embarrassed at their findings.

Of course, there is no merit pay for outstanding individuals and, like the elementary and secondary teachers, after they have achieved tenure, there is little that can be done about those that cannot pull their own weight.

Let us consider efficiency in terms of dollars and cents. Suppose your son wants to become an architect and you must use your own funds plus the Liberty School voucher to pay all costs. Assume you live in the Detroit area.

There are three Schools of Architecture in Michigan, all of them accredited. Here are your choices:

- Lawrence Institute of Technology, with 4,000 students, half of these part-time. Located in suburban Detroit, the Institute has survived for many years without public money. Runs on a no-nonsense basis with professors on 16 contact hours per week (the highest I have heard of). In addition, they utilize the services of 125 part-time instructors, who work full time for high-technology industries in the Detroit area. These instructors are up to date on the latest in the real world of their specialty; they are enthusiastic about the opportunity to teach and the cost to Lawrence is minimal.

  The physical plant is used from early in the morning till late at night. Cost (73-74 dollars), $1060.00 per year. For this amount you get no campus life, no sports, just an opportunity to learn and receive the all-important degree.

- University of Detroit, a Jesuit-operated institution where professors average 12 contact hours per week. Tuition at this respected, 100-year-old institution is $2180.00 per year. Minimum sports and campus life.
- University of Michigan, a public institution in Ann Arbor, 35 miles from Detroit. If the student had to pay the total cost and the costs were at the national average (they are probably more), the cost would be $4100.00 per year. Our student would get lots of campus life, sports, and extra-curricular programs.

With the present distribution of funds, your student can attend the University of Michigan for $500.00 per year plus room and board. The total cost would be in the neighborhood of $500.00 to the student and $3600.00 (national average) to the taxpayers for a total of $4100.00 per year. Living at home and attending Lawrence ($1060) or the University of Detroit ($2180.00) does not seem very attractive under these circumstances. But if we gave the money to the student instead of the institution, then Lawrence becomes most attractive.

Critics will ask, "How can you compare the costs of a limited purpose trade school like Lawrence with those of a diverse organization like U. of M.; which has programs from medicine to nuclear physics, from astronomy to forestry?" That's a good question! First, let's consider why the student goes to college. He wants to get a degree in architecture and learn enough about the profession to become employed by an architectural firm. So a student who had a free choice would probably call the personnel office of 10 large architectural firms in the Detroit area and ask, "All other things being equal, which graduate would you prefer, U of M, U of D, or LIT?" Graduates of Lawrence are frequently preferred over the other two.

In no case would they reject a graduate of Lawrence. There is no clear-cut preference for any school, but were the student to pay the entire cost, and unless the student's family were wealthy, LIT would be the choice by most students. And these are the results of an actual phone survey.

As to that part of the question applying to medicine, nuclear physics, astronomy and forestry, our student is not interested in those subjects. Nor, the way huge institutions like U of M are organized, is he likely to rub shoulders with any students or instructors in those fields. So no claim can be made that our student will be "broadened" by the experience. In fact, universities with a broad curriculum like U of M's often operate departments that are economically unfeasible. Possibly there should be only a few departments of nuclear physics in the whole country, rather than one in every state.

Contrast this with LIT's experience several years ago with a course in Civil Engineering. The enrollment dropped below the minimum break-even point, so the management did the prudent thing and terminated the course. Had the school been publicly financed, experience tells us that Civil Engineering would be very much a part of the curriculum today.

There is no intent here to say that large institutions like the University of Michigan, Ohio State University, and other large state-operated institutions of higher education are undesirable. We can be confident that they have much to offer. What is important is that students should not be compelled to attend by the way we distribute our tax money. With the tax funds going to the student instead of the institution, he will be free to choose among the many alternatives that are available in private and public schools, in his home state or in another state, even a foreign country. At the same time those colleges and universities presently not sharing in the public's funds will have an opportunity to continue to serve. They have much to contribute to our society. Well-managed institutions will survive, others will fail. But our primary objective, that students will receive the best education possible, will be met. This is, of course, why we taxpayers provide the funds to begin with.

In the next few years, our present methods of financing higher education will be under increasing strain as the same enrollment declines now troubling elementary and secondary education move into the college age group. Entering freshmen in institutions of higher education stood at 1.27 million in 1965. The peak in 1976 or 1977 will be around 1.53 million. By 1985, it will be back down to 1.24 million, a drop of 19% (U. S. Office of Education). And it could become even worse when graduates find that they cannot get the jobs they expect as the result of their degrees, or if the prohibition against using degrees as an exclusive credentialing device as recommended in the next chapter becomes a reality, and without a Viet Nam war to encourage the use of college attendance to evade draft calls.

Earlier, in Chapter 3, we discussed a way to distribute the tax money we now give to colleges and universities to the student instead of the institutions. The annual Liberty School vouchers suggested at the elementary and secondary level are not the answer because of the diversity of spending options available to students at the higher education level. A better way may be to give each student, when he reaches 18 years of age, an entitlement, representing his fair share of the total tax dollars spent on higher education. The student would then be free to make choices among public and private colleges and universities, career-oriented schools, etc.

Since not all of those reaching the age of eighteen would

use any or all of these funds, the amount of the entitlement could be adjusted upward, after a statistical study. For instance, the total amount we now spend in federal, state and local funds is now (74-75) *about 18.7 billions.* This excludes funds for sponsored research and room and board. About 4.1 million persons became eighteen that year so the "pie" divides up into slices of $4400 for each individual. But only 43% of those four million enter college and only 23% stay to get a four year degree. More than half would not use any of this benefit. We can assume that for our purposes, a statistical study would indicate a figure of aroung $14,000 per student.* This amount need not cause any increase in taxes at any level. The $14,000.00 entitlement might actually result in a *decrease* in the tax load as enrollment declines.

The entitlement of $14,000.00 would be a lifelong asset, rather than restricted to a certain period of his life. He could use this entitlement at any time in his life, for any educational purpose. The student could buy many different types of education. As in the earlier example, he could attend the Lawrence Institute of Technology, the University of Detroit, the University of Michigan, a community college,

$$* \quad \frac{18.7 \text{ Billion}}{43\% \times 4.1 \text{ Million}} = 10,600.00$$

$$\frac{18.7 \text{ Billion}}{23\% \times 4.1 \text{ Million}} = 19,830.00$$

$$\text{Average} = 15,215.00$$

But we reduce this figure to $14,000 to be on the safe side because the 43% to 23% is not a straight line decline. This also makes allowance for other errors caused by technique. The resulting figure is on the conservative side.

Population Figures from Bureau of Census Current
Population Report Series II

private or religious colleges, vocational colleges, correspondence schools, foreign colleges, etc.

If the cost of our student's higher education program
exceeds the $14,000.00, he could rely on his own or family
funds, scholarships or student loans. Colleges and universities voluntarily joining the Liberty plan could be required
to provide scholarships in some relation to their income
from gifts and endowments, thus providing similar leverage
for the poor as described for elementary and secondary
schools charging an add-on tuition. Since the private, or
independent schools, receive 26.2% of their budgets from
gifts and endowments, this leverage can be substantial.
The independents' 26.2% compares with only 2.5% in the
public universities.

Critics will say that the universal application of an across
the board entitlement for students of all families, regardless
of income, would tend to subsidize the rich. But when
you consider that students from wealthy families will apply
their entitlement to the more expensive institutions, which
in turn will be required to provide scholarships for the
poor, this inequity will be self-correcting. In addition, we
avoid the need for a bureaucracy to determine who is entitled
and who is not.

The entitlement could be used for board and room,
or for any normal expenses involved in higher education.
Graduate schools would be included. To start the program
off, nineteen, twenty, and twenty-one (and on up) year-olds
would have entitlements reduced in proportion to their age.
Otherwise an unfair situation would exist during the first
few years.

The object of the Liberty plan is not to spend more
on education but to reroute the funds through the students
to the institution. Will the availability of such a substantial
entitlement for higher education inflate the use of tax funds

beyond their present use? An effective way to control excessive, or frivolous, use of these funds would be to require that 25% of any educational expenditure be paid by the student and 75% by the entitlement. Scholarships should be available from the institution for students who are unable to raise the 25%. As discussed earlier, the amount of the scholarship funds available from each institution can be related to its income from gifts and endowments.

What about expensive professional education like medical schools? Under our present procedure, governments provide massive amounts of money to medical schools, which in turn select and train future doctors. Sometimes publicly funded medical schools have astronomical costs, bearing little relation to costs in prudently run independent schools.

John R. Silber in a recent Atlantic Monthly article speaks of one state medical school where the costs, including capital amortization, are a staggering $160,000.00 *per year, per student.* Under the present arrangement, taxpayers are placed in the curious position of providing free preparation for a profession which shows extremely high lifetime earnings. This is analogous to a government buying the machinery and plant necessary for a manufacturer to start a profitable business.

With the Liberty plan, medical students would receive the same basic entitlement as all other young persons. Medical schools would receive directly no tax funds except for specified research projects. Assuming the student and his family are unable to pay the added costs of a medical school, government-insured interest-bearing loans should be available to cover these costs. Thus doctors themselves would be paying the "price of admission" for admission into a high earning profession.

Milton Friedman has suggested an alternative to loans

to students for professional education. He suggests that individuals and financial institutions might buy a share in the student's future earnings. The investors would have high earnings from successful borrowers, sufficient to make up for losses on those who do not fulfill their investment potential.

Each state would have a different higher education entitlement, according to what amount of tax money had been previously devoted to this purpose. Only the federal portion of these funds would be the same in all states. The amount of the entitlement could increase with inflation or with changes in public policy. For example, if a student used $7,000.00 of his $14,000.00, then left school and returned in five years, he might find that the basic entitlement had increased to $18,000.00. In this case, he would still be entitled to half, or $9,000.00.

States would necessarily have to establish a residency requirement to qualify students for this benefit. Federal coordination might be needed where a student's family has moved frequently. Thus, the total entitlement might be allocated against several states.

In elementary and secondary education, we proposed that parents elect boards of education to run the newly independent and formerly "public" schools. How would the presently politically operated public college and universities be controlled? One means would be to elect regents from among those who have an interest in the continued successful operation of the institution. Among the interested parties are the alumni, the faculty, the students and local citizens. Since state-supported schools are the major industry in many college towns, these citizens would have a vital interest in continued operation. Thus we might have an elected board of regents consisting of one member from the faculty, three from the alumni, two from the community and one from the student body. Regents from the faculty would be forbidden to vote on faculty salary or working conditions. Terms would be staggered, to insure continuity.

16. The Diploma Curtain

"The facts of this case demonstrate the inadequacy of broad and general testing devices as well as the infirmity of using diplomas or degrees as fixed measures of capability. History is filled with examples of men and women who rendered highly effective performance without the conventional badges of accomplishment in terms of certificates, diplomas or degrees. Diplomas and tests are useful servants, but Congress had mandated the common-sense proposition that they are not to become the masters of reality"

Chief Justice Burger;
Supreme Court of the United States;
Griggs vs. Duke Power, 1971.

THIS DECISION, APPLYING to a case of racial discrimination under Title VII of the Civil Rights Act of 1964, may forecast the end of a most serious type of discrimination, affecting more people than racial discrimination. The obvious discrimination practiced in government and industry by requiring degrees that bear little or no relation to the job would seem to be an area ripe for action by the American Civil Liberties Union.

Colleges and universities, in conjunction with employing governments and businesses, have created a demand for educational services that in many cases does not reflect reality. A college degree is required for employment and promotion in many jobs where educational level attained has little relation to the tasks performed. It is not true that an individual cannot succeed in life without a college degree. But it is true that he succeeds with great difficulty unless he has the certificate which indicates he put in the time, whether or not he received an education. This situation has come about because we have made education into a state religion and permitted ourselves to be convinced by its high priests that it is essential. We must break the connection between the degree and competence for employment or promotion. Competency indicated by a certificate which proves we spent so many years in a particular school means little except that we were docile enough to permit our incarceration.

What do undergraduate students and their parents who struggle to finance them want from a college or university? After all the rhetoric about quality education, outstanding faculty, community of scholars, etc., what they really want—the vast majority—is a degree. The young person with a degree finds that he has access to choices in business, civil service, professions, etc. But until he gets that all important degree, he has few career choices. A fact of life, regrettable but true.

As the gatekeepers to economic success, some educators reason that, having been successful in making a bachelor's degree mandatory for the most minor jobs, they can now sell the idea that a master's degree should be required for something with a little more status, thus producing an ever-increasing demand for higher education and for professors. In other words, more is automatically better. The absurdity of this trend has become evident in the present underemployment of Ph.D. holders as taxi drivers, mechanics, etc.

The serious nature of this discrimination is well described by Peter Drucker:[18]

> The most serious impact of the long years of schooling is, however, the 'diploma curtain' between those

with degrees and those without. It threatens to cut
society in two for the first time in American history.
We are in danger of confining access to opportunity
to those—still less than half of our young people—
who have stayed in school beyond high school, and
particularly to those who have finished college. Even
ordinary jobs are increasingly reserved for those who
have at least finished high school. We thus are
denying full citizenship in the knowledge society
to the large group—15 to 20 percent perhaps—who
stopped before they could get a high school diploma.
And we are sharply curtailing access to opportunities
for half the population—the ones who don't attend
college.

This is not only new in American history. It
is singularly stupid. The great strength of American
society throughout our history lay in our willingness
to use human resources, in our willingness to put
ability, ambition, and dedication to productive use
wherever it arose. We never fully lived up to this
principle. We certainly did not live up to it with
respect to women. And we disregarded it entirely
in the case of the black man. But never before did
we deny it explicitly as we are now doing.

By denying opportunity to those without higher
education, we are denying access to contribution
and performance to a large number of people of
superior ability, intelligence, and capacity to
achieve. There is not much correlation between
ability to do well in school and ability to perform
in life and work (except perhaps in academic work).
There is no reason to believe that the diploma
certifies to much more than that the holder has sat
a long time.

The diploma curtain even pervades the military. During
all of our recent wars, including both World Wars, officers

were commissioned from the ranks and promoted based on demonstrated competence. Once the shooting stopped, officers were told they could not continue to serve their country as officers unless they had a degree! During wars, we want people competent to destroy the enemy. After the war is over, we want officers with credentials, not good fighters but officers with good taste. It would seem that we risk the security of our country on dubious personnel practices.

More on how we have allowed the degree to degenerate into a pervasive system of discrimination and monopoly power for educators is provided by Alexander Mood[19] in *The Future of Higher Education*:

> Parents are correct in their belief that there is a job discrimination against those without a degree. The discrimination is so rampant as to be almost unbelievable. A few years ago I helped carry out a survey of a large federal agency to explore the extent to which there might be discrimination against employees because of their race or sex. There turned out to be little discrimination on either of those two counts but there was absolute and total discrimination with respect to lack of a college degree. Civil Service Grade 11 is toward the middle of the hierarchy of government positions; in this particular agency not a single person without a degree occupied Grade 11 or any higher-level position. Degreeless persons were held below that grade no matter how able, no matter how long they served the agency; and some of them were extremely able. On the other hand, young fellows with degrees went whistling right through those lower levels and into grades 12, 13, and sometimes 14 before they were 35 years old. An amazing aspect of the whole business was that there was little bitterness about this kind of

discrimination among the degreeless persons, even among those who knew quite well that their ability far exceeded that of persons who had passed them by. They had been brainwashed by our society and our educational system into believing that they had condemned themselves forever, many years ago in their youth, by not getting more education, and hence that there was some modicum of reasonableness in the outrages that government personnel policies were perpetrating on them. Similarly, youths, who are often denied employment even at the unskilled labor level because they do not have a high school diploma, often tend to blame themselves for not finishing high school rather than the employer for practicing unwarranted discrimination.

Thus higher education as a nationwide institution has maneuvered itself into the position that every youth with any ambition at all must pay tribute to it if he is to have a chance of realizing his ambition. And it is a huge tribute: a large sum of money and four years filled with much drudgery. From this point of view it is no wonder that many young people hate higher education: it is a trap from which they cannot escape. In the past there were escape routes of a sort; one could go into business, for example, without a degree and achieve some kind of social status by working at it diligently. Now the escape routes are closed off: you must have a degree these days to become an insurance salesman. People detest that kind of coercion; the role of gatekeeper to employment opportunities will continue to generate increasing hatred of higher education; it is already a strong contributing factor to the ferment in higher education today.

If employers' requirement of a high school diploma is rejected by the courts, will many students drop out?

Will master's degrees and doctorates be ruled out as an employers' credentialing device for upper level jobs? Will requirements of degrees in the teaching profession for certification or promotion be ruled out? Can persons without degrees become teachers? In the Griggs case and at least seven others decided in 1970, 1971 and 1972, the Supreme Court is writing answers to these questions. What will happen to education?

The elimination of schools' monopoly power over access to jobs will provide new freedom for students and education. After losing the false demand for their services, schools will begin to fill the many unmet knowledge needs of young and old. Within schools themselves, the phony requirements of degrees for certification and promotion will hopefully be replaced by ability and demonstrated performance on the job.

In addition to providing a free choice of schools and some elements of a competitive market system, education will not move very far or very fast into the future unless we eliminate this false reliance on diplomas and degrees to sustain the market for education services. It is essential that this diploma curtain be parted if education and schools are to move forward into the future.

The Liberty plan suggests federal legislation outlawing requirements by both public and private employers for diplomas or degrees as the sole source of credentials for employment and promotion. That is not to say that diplomas or degrees cannot be *one* route to jobs and promotion. But there must be other avenues open to the self-taught or simply those with strong determination to succeed. Discrimination is indicated if these avenues do not exist.

17. The Future of Education

". . . our schools face backward towards a dying system rather than forward to the emerging new society. Their vast energies are applied to cranking out Industrial Man—people tooled for survival in a system that will be dead before they are" [Alvin Toffler, *Future Shock*[20]]

FORECASTING THE FUTURE is a precarious business, whatever the line of endeavor. With education, we can only speculate based on the technology that now exists but has not yet been applied. But some direction must be provided in order to accomplish anything, so we must forecast, and, when our errors become evident, try again.

The staff of the Wall Street Journal wrote a little book called *Here Comes Tomorrow, Living and Working in the Year 2000.* It is actually a compilation of articles published in the Journal in 1966 and 1967. Here is part of what is said about education:

> Enrollments at all levels will soar. Census Bureau forecasts indicate the United States school-age population (5 to 24) will swell to more than 125 million by the year 2000 from 70.2 million in early 1967. The proportion of this group actually in the classroom will climb because of the surge in college undergraduate and graduate study. Moreover, the young people will be joined in the pursuit of education by rising numbers of adults.

How wrong can you be in seven years? The school age population was actually declining at the time the articles were being written, and will decline further. It appears likely that the school age population will not again reach the 70.2 million before the year 2000. The forecast of 125 million is off by close to 50%!

Demographers (population experts) do not have a very good track record. In the 30's, they were forecasting that the U.S. population of 130 million was stable and we could anticipate no growth in our economy or population. Until a few years ago, the sons of the 1930's experts had been forecasting a population explosion with standing room only from sea to shining sea. Now the pendulum is swinging the other way and we can expect some of this same group will soon be urging baby bonuses to stabilize our population, and that may not be a bad idea!

HEW's Office of Education forecasts a continuing drop in K–12 enrollment from 49.7 million in 1974 to 45 million in 1982. This is based on the Census Bureau's projections, series "E". The actual continued drop in birth rates could make even these figures too generous. We described earlier how enrollment in higher education, after peaking in 1976-77, will decline 19% into 1985.

It would seem to this nonexpert that both figures may be high. The continued success of the women's liberation movement and availability of reliable birth control methods will continue to reduce birth rates to unheard of levels. At the same time, the ideas (which are not new) expressed in this book about schools and degrees having lost their luster, will work to further decrease enrollment, particularly in institutions of higher education. The foregoing could well encourage prospective educators to switch to another line of endeavor. And we hope it will, for those who in the past found in education a shelter from the trials and tribulations of the real world.

But for those who like to pioneer in exciting new things, education can be like the space program was in the 60's.

There is one big IF: If we give school money to parents and students, not schools, while at the same time we unleash education by outlawing discrimination by degree or diploma.

The possibility of parents with fewer children spending more money on education offers a marketing opportunity that schools have failed to realize. The way schools are now organized, we effectively prevent parents from spending more money on children's educations.

In any industry, management looks for opportunities to expand sales by increasing the unit sale. In automobiles, they call it *more car per car.* Educators have such an opportunity now. It includes more employment for teachers, increased sales of learning devices, books, charts, etc. Will they accept the challenge?

People of all ages will seek more of what educators have to offer because they thirst for knowledge, and they will need vastly more to live and work. At the same time, the new breed of educators will make it fun, not a distasteful chore, to learn.

We all know about the success of Sesame Street and the Electric Company for children. Learning was presented so imaginatively that young viewers were attracted from other points on the dial. Can we do the same for secondary students and adults? Of course, we already are! Examples are the superb series by Lord Kenneth Clark, "Civilization," and Alistair Cooke's "America."

With the liberation of education you will no longer see the professor on your TV screen at 6:00 A.M. giving a lecture to his TV class in the same way he and his predecessors have done in the lecture hall at the university for hundreds of years. In the future, the subject being taught will be illustrated with the instructor's voice in the background. Every illustration, every word, every gesture, every sound will be planned to enhance effective learning.

What's more, you won't have to rise at 6:00 A.M. to get the professor's lecture, but you can have it at *your* convenience on videotape, videodisc, or cable TV. Not only will you learn at your own time but at your speed and your place, at home, at school or at work.

Teachers will counsel students on which tapes to use, answer questions, offer encouragement. Master teachers will plan the production of tapes in conjunction with TV technicians, using every modern technique.

Cost? A 30 minute tape on elementary mathematics might cost $150,000.00 or more but wide distribution and use can cut the cost to pennies per student. At the same time, the learning efficiency can be doubled or tripled. Learning materials like this can be produced by entrepreneurs, who may sell copies or be rewarded on a royalty-per-use basis.

In *The Future of Higher Education,* Alexander Mood[19] suggests that we rearrange some of our attitudes and expectations:

(1) The vast majority of students would attend college as full-time students for only one year, instead of four or two.

(2) Additional higher education would be a part-time activity extending over one's lifetime.

(3) Almost every youth would attend college for one year, whether or not he or she had graduated from high school.

(4) The roles of residential and community colleges would be essentially reversed: the one year of full-time attendance would be at a residential college, and the part-time lifelong learning would lie more in the domain of the community college.

(5) The year of residence for those who do not now go to college would be financed by the public subsidy that now supports students who attend college for more than one year.

Once education is freed from its anachronistic organization and is no longer a monopoly collector of tolls on the bridge to economic success, its future may be largely electronic. Included will be computers, video tapes or discs, and most importantly, cable television.

Two items now in the testing stage from American Telephone and Telegraph are the Electronic Blackboard and a Lecture-Conference Hookup. The Electronic Blackboard allows an instructor to write on his blackboard at one location. Simultaneously, the same information can appear on another blackboard anywhere in the world.

This development can be used in conjunction with the Conference Hookup. It will permit a guest lecturer from UCLA to deliver his talk at the University of Chicago, without leaving California. Students, provided with individual microphones, can discuss the subject with the distant lecturer.

In the work mentioned earlier, Alexander Mood's *The Future of Higher Education*,[19] the author speculates on video cassettes being used in the home TV set. The cassettes would be available on every subject from A to Z.

The "Video University" would provide consulting services to students, provide a library of the tapes, and administer any tests necessary to certify the student's competence gained through his home learning, for whatever purpose. Such an approach need not be limited to higher education but might be used to some extent at all levels.

This idea would provide equality of educational opportunity, regardless of age; the learning schedule would fit the student's spare time; cost would be minimal; students would be free of artificial limits such as requirements for a high school diploma, or other prerequisites, and freedom from psychological barriers which now inhibit adults from attending schools. This approach could supplant correspondence schools, which have not been great successes due to inability to hold the student's interest.

There are fantastic possibilities in the developing cable TV industry. Not only for education but two-way sight, sound, and data communications; for shopping; paying bills; and even voting. Homes beyond the range of economical cable installation would be served by microwave links, satellites or even laser beams. The technology is available now for all of this, but its utilization is stymied by politics and the question of ownership, public vs. private.

For education, the effect will be revolutionary. Students at home or in school could retrieve virtually any book, video tape or audiovisual material, with the display on their TV screen. This home information system would provide an electronic printout, should you wish to copy pages from a book or any other learning resource.

Access would be provided to the Video Library mentioned earlier; to computers programmed for instruction; and to live teachers at distant schools. Despite the man-made obstacles in its way, this development should begin to affect education in the late 70's with full application in the early 80's.

18. Conclusions

SHOULD YOUR STATE move toward liberating its schools, the parents must be alert to the tendency of bureaucracies to smother new ideas in red tape; be ready to reject cries for more money; avoid participation of the federal government, except for funds channeled through the vouchers; and strike down insulting insinuations that any parent, rich or poor, black or white, is incompetent to choose a school for his child.

Since these proposals would change the way of life of so many people, they are sure to receive much criticism. The critics will be highly vocal and, if educators, will have access to the media to a greater extent than do ordinary parents, to whom these ideas appeal.

Regarding educational reform, here is another appropriate quotation from Alexander Mood's *The Future of Higher Education:*[19]

> Reform is most unlikely to come from within the educational establishment; it is a well-entrenched bureaucracy with a mission altogether palatable to and appreciated by the general public. It is a most comfortable bureaucracy whose members enjoy the ultimate in job security, a comfortable income, and considerable social status. They are not about to rock that boat. The laymen who have the responsibility to see to it that the bureaucracy serves the public have shown few signs that they are going to rock the boat. I refer to school board members, trustees, legislators, and various state and local officials. They see no great reward in trying to discipline a bureaucracy which, by and large, has

a good public image and hence substantial political power. Further, they feel somewhat inadequate, as laymen, to confront the educational experts in the very arena in which they are expert.

Our courts seem to be the only agency that can knock the artificial credential prop from under our educational system and bring it down to the sound foundation of education for its own sake.

If one or more of the ideas outlined in this book is important to your family, then your state legislator is the place to begin. Action is needed now. With our present school organization the crisis can only escalate.

Legislation will be required to make the Liberty School idea a reality. Some of the groups involved in education will be opposed to some parts of the legislation, in favor of others. A really workable program will require all of the legislation, although some of it may be enacted initially to encourage the temporary solution, as described in Chapter 13. In the listing below, items A through F would fall in this category.

A. Relieve all public school districts or systems of territorial responsibilities and limitations. This would permit public school systems to seek students or to operate schools beyond their present boundaries.

B. Permit portability of per-pupil expenditures from one school district to another. Short of a full voucher system, this would encourage and permit students to choose a school in an adjoining district. Forbid racial discrimination in enrollment policies.

C. Prohibit school administrators and/or teachers from conspiring together to reduce the competitive effects of any open enrollment or voucher plan and provide penalties. As the Rand Corporation's study of the Alum rock demonstration points out, school people will conspire to prevent competition. (Chapter 2)

D. Permit the payment by parents of add-on tuition exceeding state and local tax funds. At the same time, require that should a school system use this method of financing it must have at least 5% of its enrollment in scholarships for the poor. No racial quotas should be required, but no racial discrimination in the selection of scholarship applicants should be permitted.

E. Eliminate the minimum number of school days per year. Days lost from a planned program due to strikes shall proportionately reduce voucher money. Permit teachers and other school people to strike.

F. Transfer the control of school districts to parent-elected boards, rather than boards elected by citizens at large.

G. Eliminate all state laws regarding schools and education. This action would eliminate certification and tenure, while permitting a completely new organization.

H. Require elementary and secondary schools to provide instruction in only the basic 3R's and citizenship. Provide for achievement tests to measure schools' accomplishments of these basic objectives, and to help parents judge schools.

I. Set up qualifications for schools regarding financial stability, and to prevent fraudulent schools. Provide machinery for schools or groups of schools to secede from large school systems.

J. Provide for the phasing in of nonpublic schools and minimum regulations to insure that school voucher money is used only for education. This would prevent a church school for example, using the voucher money to replace the roof on the church.

K. Provide for the Liberty School Sector; its initial ownership of public school property; terms of sale to independent school systems; disposal of surplus; transportation and other matters.

L. Reorganize distribution of funds through vouchers with only very narrowly defined amounts to go to the state Department of Education. Provide extra vouchers for students with learning disabilities.

M. Reorganize institutions of higher education, changing their governance and making them nonprofit independent associations. Set up the machinery for students to draw their entitlement for use at any approved educational institution in the world. Provide for secondary students to use a portion of their entitlement in vocational schools.

N. Reduce the school-leaving age to 14 after the few years necessary to set up programs such as a Conservation Corps to attract these young people.

O. Federal legislation should include:

(1) Provision for distribution of federal funds now going to a state, to go through the voucher machinery if the state elects.

(2) Gradual reduction of education activities of the Federal Government as states set up Liberty programs.

(3) Means to forbid discrimination by diploma or degree, with penalties.

* * *

We have seen how the Liberty School plan would give the taxpayer's money to the parents (or students of higher education) instead of the schools. This would be in the form of vouchers good only for educational purposes. The idea has a number of advantages. Benefits will appeal to widely different groups for various reasons. These include:

- Improving education by providing a choice of schools with different concepts of teaching to better serve each child's unique characteristics of emotional makeup, intelligence, aptitudes, family background and learning style.
- Providing access to any school in the state by any child, rich or poor, black or white, thus furthering racial integration without forced busing.
- Permitting optional moral or religious instruction in all schools and providing financial support for religious schools, without any increase in taxes.
- Allowing teachers to choose schools that have teaching philosophies compatible with their own. Superior teachers can be paid more for outstanding work.
- Enabling, through the add-on tuition feature, additional non-tax funds to flow into improved schools, providing jobs for thousands of now unemployed teachers.
- Teacher militancy seeking to dominate schools can be redirected to cooperation with school managers in order to satisfy parent customers.
- Schools with falling enrollment will be closed by parental choice, not administrative edict.
- The competitive climate will improve the efficiency, effectiveness and consumer responsiveness of schools.
- The gross inequity in the way we distribute funds for higher education will be eliminated. Cost effectiveness of these public institutions will be immeasurably improved.

- Putting an end to the serious discrimination we practice by using diplomas and degrees as credentials for employment and promotion. By freeing schools from the support of this artificial market, they can respond to the unmet knowledge needs of young and old.
- Increasing personal freedom through choice, to satisfy unique student needs. Thus we put schools under the control of using parents and students instead of political conformity.
- Opening the door to an exciting future for education and educators, through technological advances and ongoing organizational evolution.

All change creates problems. And the way to judge whether changes are improvements is whether or not the change solves more problems than it creates. The Liberty plan will solve far more problems than are created.

Do we have the fortitude to grasp this opportunity? Yes: If we, as a free people, can allow diversity and freedom of choice, then constructive agreement about how we operate schools can be attained.

Notes

1. *Inequality.* Christopher Jencks. New York: Basic Books, Inc., 1972.

2. *Capitalism and Freedom.* Milton Friedman. Chicago: University of Chicago Press, 1962.

3. *The Greening of the High School.* New York: Educational Facilities Laboratory, 1973.

4. Gallup, 1973.

5. HEW's national statistics indicate that we spent $3724.00 per full time equivalent student at public institutions of higher education in the 1973-74 school year. This figure includes community colleges and tuition of about $500.00.

But, to calculate a more accurate figure, we must include a portion of the capital outlay these institutions make for new buildings, replacement and rehabilitation. The total is 3.1 billion dollars. Divide this by 5,491,000 students and we see that the figure is $550.00 per full time equivalent student. For some reason, educators are reluctant to include buildings in their cost figures. Yet buildings do have to be bought, replaced or rehabilitated, in order for schools to operate.

This brings the total to $4274.00. One final adjustment must be made. Some of this total includes funds spent for dormitories, cafeterias, etc. According to HEW's statisticians the amount spent on these items is poorly reported and some of it is returned in the form of fees or sales of meals, etc. An educated guess would deduct $174.00 per student. This makes the final figure $4100.00, including $500.00 tuition.

Figures are extracted from Projections of Educational Statistics to 1983-84, 1974 edition, Dept. of Health, Education and Welfare, NCES 75-209.

6. *The Reform of Secondary Education.* Copyrighted © by the Institute for Development of Educational Activities, Inc. National Commission on the Reform of Secondary Education, established by the Charles F. Kettering Foundation. New York: McGraw-Hill, 1973.

7. *Things to Come.* Herman Kahn and B. Bruce-Briggs. Copyright © 1972 by the Hudson Institute. New York: MacMillan Company, 1972.

8. March, 1974.

9. Projections of Educational Statistics to 1983-4, 1974 Edition, Department of Health, Education and Welfare, NCES 75-209.

10. Excerpted from *The School Book* by Neil Postman and Charles Weingartner. Copyright © 1973 by Neil Postman and Charles Weingartner. Used with permission of Delacorte Press. New York: 1973.

11. *Crisis in the Classroom.* Charles E. Silberman. Copyright © by Charles E. Silberman, 1970. New York: Random House, 1970.

12. Reprinted from *Here Comes Tomorrow!.* Copyright © Dow Jones Books, 1967. All rights reserved.

13. Excerpted from the Wall Street Journal, with permission.

14. *A Public School Voucher Demonstration: The First Year at* Alum Rock, Summary and Conclusions. Santa Monica, California: Rand Corporation, Report #R-1495/1-NIE, June, 1974.

15. *Public Schools of Choice.* Mario D. Fantini. New York: Simon and Schuster, 1973.

16. *What's Happened to Teacher.* Myron Brenton. New York: Coward-McCann, 1970.

17. *This Beats Working for a Living.* Professor X. New Rochelle, N.Y.: Arlington House, 1973. Copyright © by Arlington House, New Rochelle, New York. All rights reserved. Used with permission.

18. *The Age of Discontinuity.* Peter F. Drucker. New York: Harper and Row, 1968.

19. Quoted with the permission of the Carnegie Commission on Higher Education from *The Future of Higher Education: Some Speculations and Suggestions* by Alexander M. Mood, published by McGraw-Hill Book Co. Copyright © 1973 by The Carnegie Foundation for the Advancement of Teaching.

20. *Future Shock.* Alvin Toffler. Copyright © by Alvin Toffler. New York: Random House, 1970.

Index